CRIME AND BUSINESS

CRIME AND BUSINESS

What You Should Know About the Infiltration of Crime Into Business — And of Business Into Crime

Edited by Michael Gartner

Introduction ...

Some big businessmen are criminals. Most big criminals are businessmen. To the discomfort of law-enforcement officials and to the dismay of the public, business and crime are becoming more and more intertwined. A racketeer will put his booty into legitimate business. A businessman might put his profits into illegitimate operations.

"In keeping with modern trends, and apart from their income-producing criminal activities, racketeers have been making increased efforts to improve their image and to legitimize and better utilize their ill-gotten wealth. In this secondary role, they are adopting a changeover from rough mob-type operations to the smooth business-like approach," a March 1970 report by the New York State Commission of Investigation concluded. "What is being attempted is to present the new look of the racketeer—a would-be businessman."

The Wall Street Journal, the nation's second largest daily newspaper and a paper with a special interest in business, has from time to time chronicled the ties between these two elements of our society. Now, for the first time, the best of these stories have been gathered into a book.

This is not an entertaining book. It shows how criminals have muscled in on legitimate businesses, how the public often deals—albeit unknowingly—with organized crime. It profiles some criminals who are businessmen—and takes some long hard looks at some businessmen who are criminals. It shows how criminals operate in nearly every area—from the unsubtle bank robbers (there are an average of seven bank holdups each day) to the Las Vegas mobsters (those corporations that moved into Las Vegas to clean it up kept many known mobsters on their payrolls).

The book takes some close looks at the small-time as well as the big-time victimizers. Here are the Terrible Williamsons, a nomadic clan of Scottish con men. Here are a surprising number of affluent students, stealing whatever they need from their campus bookstores. Here are some rugged lumbermen of the Pacific Northwest, poaching valuable logs. And here are some modern-day rustlers, stealing costly animals from zoos and animal farms.

But here, too, is Meyer Lansky, perhaps the most powerful leader of organized crime in America. He has so few worries and such legitimate fronts that FBI agents who tail him have discovered that whenever their car starts to fall behind he slows down to let them catch up. Meyer Lansky is not a killer; he's an executive.

And here is Louis Wolfson, an executive who once controlled a couple of huge corporations and who tried to capture control of Montgomery Ward. Louis Wolfson was charged in a criminal action for violation of securities laws, and Louis Wolfson ended up in jail. On the eve of his move to jail, he sat down with a Wall Street Journal reporter and talked about himself and business. "You've got more crooks in Wall Street than in any other industry I've ever seen," he said.

Along the way, Wall Street Journal reporters have come upon some rather engaging criminals. They tell of Machine Gun Molly, the best of the bank robbers in Montreal (where bank robbing seems to be Everyman's hobby), of Richard A., a transvestite check forger also known as Mary A., a bosomy blond. And of Sammy Amalu, a king, philosopher—and thief.

But these people are all criminals, part of the crime net that costs the good citizens of this country billions of dollars a year. It's estimated that organized crime alone takes in $50 billion annually from gambling, narcotics, usurious loans, prostitution and the numbers game. It then reinvests much of this in thousands of businesses, ranging from electronics to trucking, from banking to construction.

How does this happen? Who's to blame? Wall Street Journal investigative reporter Stanley Penn, a winner of the Pulitzer Prize, grapples with some of these questions in the final piece in this book. But there are, of course, no easy answers.

—MICHAEL GARTNER
Editor

The stories in this book first appeared in The Wall Street Journal between early 1968 and late 1970. They have not been changed to take into account any subsequent events.

Contents

CONTENTS

CONTENTS

CRIME AND BUSINESS

Muscling In

MURRAY Packing Co. became a dead duck the moment Joseph Pagano was named president in 1961.

The Weinberg and Newman families that controlled the Bronx meat processor seemed powerless to control their new president. Testimony in Federal District Court in New York reveals he bought large quantities of supplies on credit, then made quick sales to customers at cut-rate prices. He pocketed nearly $750,000 of Murray funds, the testimony indicates. The company, some $1.3 million in debt, went bankrupt a short time later.

The owners didn't know it, but they had turned over control to the Mafia.

A 1964 Senate subcommittee report on racketeering identified Pagano, who was sent to prison for his now-celebrated activity at Murray, as a member of the feared Mafia gang, or "family," of the late Vito Genovese. The family operates in the New York-New Jersey area and is one of the largest of the more than 20 similar Mafia groups around the country, law enforcement officials say.

It was unusual that the Mafia could get control of a legitimate business like Murray, but it is becoming less unusual. By various methods, organized crime is infiltrating a growing number of legitimate businesses. According to the Justice Department, organized crime now has links with tens of thousands of businesses and businessmen in such widely ranging fields as electronics, trucking, banking, construction, real estate and food and health services.

One motive, surprisingly, is to establish a money-making front to justify the criminals' luxurious way of life. Without such a front, the Internal Revenue Service would be constantly investigating Mafia members to find out where they get the money for their high living. The front, the criminals hope, provides the answer.

The Mafia has plenty of cash to invest in these legitimate enterprises. Its yearly revenue from gambling, narcotics, usurious loans, prostitution and the numbers game has been estimated at as much as $50 billion.

How does the Mafia work its way in? There are several methods. Pagano had worked for a Murray affiliate and knew the parent firm was short of capital. According to court testimony, he told the owners that if made president he'd invest $35,000 in the firm for a one-third interest and would bring in new business through his connections in the wholesale meat field. The owners bought the deal.

Joseph Weinberg, one of the principals of Murray, found to his dismay that once gangsters get control it's difficult to force them out. Weinberg tried vainly to get Pagano to discontinue withdrawing Murray's funds for his own use, testimony indicates. "Look at the hole you are putting us into," Weinberg complained to Pagano, according to the court testimony. "Don't worry, I'll get the money back to you," Pagano lied.

Weinberg was asked in court why he didn't remove Pagano. After all, he and David Newman, another principal in the company, controlled two-thirds of Murray's stock. Weinberg's reply: "I didn't know what steps to take."

For their role in violating the Federal bankruptcy laws by defrauding creditors, Weinberg and Newman in 1965 were given 12-month and 15-month jail sentences, respectively. Pagano got a five-year sentence.

Extortion is another favorite device for gaining control of a firm. Witness the ordeal of Irving Holzman, a New York juke box distributor.

According to documents on file with the New York Court of Appeals in Albany, Mr. Holzman was asked by Salvatore Granello, a Mafioso, to meet with him at a Manhattan restaurant. There, testimony indicates, Granello got right to the point: He said Mr. Holzman should surrender one-fourth of the profits of his firm and, in return, the Mafia would see that no physical harm came to Mr. Holzman. "If at the end of a week, you have $1 left, I'll take 25 cents and you keep 75 cents," Granello explained.

When Mr. Holzman resisted, the pressure intensified. Court documents described how several men entered his home in Roslyn, N.Y., and beat up his wife. He said their married daughter, who was expecting a child, got a phone call at her home in Oyster Bay, N.Y., warning: "If your father doesn't cooperate, we'll come and kick your pregnant belly in."

But Mr. Holzman didn't cave in. He went to Nassau County District Attorney William Cahn and allowed authorities to tap his phone conversations with Granello. The mobster, convicted of an extortion plot, was given an 18-month jail term in 1967.

Because the Mafia pays no taxes on its income from illegal rackets, its members must be circumspect when they buy into legitimate businesses. They can't appear to pay more than the amount of money they could have amassed through legitimate enterprises. Otherwise, they would arouse the suspicions of the Internal Revenue Service, and that could lead to criminal charges of tax evasion.

A real estate operator who is in a position to know tells how the Mafia often dupes the IRS. "Suppose John Smith, a legitimate businessman, wants to sell a building for $1 million," he says. "The hoodlum has the money to pay for it, but he can't show he got it all legitimately. So he says to John Smith, 'We'll make the legal papers show it as a $500,000 deal, and I'll give you the other $500,000 in cash.' " The legitimate businessman agrees not to pay taxes on the cash, because if he did the IRS easily could trace the money back to the gangster.

"You take a Mafia man who owns 10 night clubs," says Ralph Salerno, a former investigator for the New York City police and now a consultant to the National Council on Crime and Delinquency. "He'll use front men as owners for nine of the clubs, and he'll show ownership for the 10th. Each club, supposedly a separate business, pays a smaller tax bill than if the Mafia man admitted ownership of all 10." He explains that under the arrangement, profits of the individual clubs are taxed at a lower rate than would prevail if the profits were pooled in one sum.

The mere charge of Mafia penetration can prove a headache to nationally known firms. In 1959, for example, Sen. John McClellan's committee on racketeering was told that Carlos Marcello, a Mafia chieftain in the New Orleans area, had a "substantial financial interest" in a motel franchised by Holiday Inns of America Inc., now one of the nation's largest motel chains.

Aaron Kohn, director of the Metropolitan Crime Commission of New Orleans, told the Senate panel that the motel—in Jefferson parish in the New Orleans metropolitan area—had been purchased in November 1958 in the names of New Orleans businessmen Roy and Frank Occhipinti and others, but that Marcello had a concealed partial interest.

Mr. Kohn says he called the alleged Marcello part-ownership to the attention of Holiday Inns management. "They were deeply concerned, and they reacted immediately," Mr. Kohn says. A Holiday Inns executive went to New Orleans to investigate, but the company took no further action. Mr. Kohn says he was informed by Holiday Inns that the Occhipintis had committed no violations of the franchise charter to provide grounds for revoking the franchise.

In 1964, the Occhipintis sold the motel, together with another Holiday Inn they controlled in New Orleans, to a group headed by Leon Poirier, a former tax accountant for Marcello. Recently, a spokesman for Mr. Poirier, asked whether Marcello was a hidden owner in the two motels, said Marcello had no financial interest in them during the period the Poirier group operated them.

Later, Holiday Inns tried to revoke the licenses of the Poirier group on the ground that the operation of the two motels didn't meet company standards. The Poirier group protested that without licenses the motels couldn't be identified as part of the national chain, and that a mortgage loan on one of the motels would be jeopardized. In a suit filed in Federal District Court in New Orleans, Mr. Poirier charged harassment and sought to block Holiday Inns from carrying out its threat.

The suit dragged on. Then came a series of transactions that ended the controversy. The Poirier group sold the two motels to a Topeka, Kan., firm. The firm, which owns other Holiday Inn motels, was acting strictly on its own initiative, maintains a Holiday Inns spokesman. Recently, Holiday Inns announced plans to buy all the motels owned by the Topeka concern. Holiday Inns insists this move isn't connected with Mr. Kohn's charge of 1959 alleging a hidden ownership by Marcello.

A Mafia-controlled enterprise, though it may operate within the law, has definite advantages over the ordinary firm against which it competes. The Mafia firm is likely to be capitalized in part with untaxed funds. Often it has no union trouble while a competitor may find itself struck by a Mafia-dominated union. And the Mafia enterprise may get bargain rates by using a Mafia-controlled trucking firm.

A hearing in New York in 1969 heard testimony suggesting that a Mafia-controlled concern can sometimes win customers away from reliable, independent firms.

A spokesman for some knife-sharpening companies told the State Commission of Investigation that steady customers switched in 1959 to a new company formed by Paul Gambino, a member of the Mafia gang headed by his brother Carlo Gambino.

To get back their customers, the independent knife sharpeners raised $175,000 and bought out the Mafia enterprise, the commission was informed. Commission members listened with skepticism as one of the customers said he didn't know that Paul Gambino was a Mafioso when he switched to the Gambino firm. He said he switched because he was offered two weeks of free service.

After listening to this and similar testimony, Commissioner Goodman A. Sarachan asked: "Does anyone really believe that an individual like Paul Gambino could persuade large chain supermarkets to switch to his company the services they were buying from well-known and reliable persons, simply by arranging to meet with executives of such chain supermarkets and offering two weeks' free service?"

The Mafia isn't averse to strong-arm tactics to promote sales. Thomas J. Mackell, district attorney in the New York borough of Queens, recently said he believed the murder of two A&P store managers and the fire bombings of 16 A&P stores and warehouses were attempts by a Mafia-controlled sales agency to force Great Atlantic & Pacific Tea Co. to buy a detergent that A&P had tested and rejected. The agency was run by the late Gene Catena, brother of Gerardo Catena, a 67-year-old Mafia chieftain in New Jersey.

How can the Mafia infiltration be stopped? Attorney General John Mitchell has suggested a novel solution: Application of the antitrust laws to break up Mafia firms that stifle competition. He believes that fines and triple-damage actions would be more effective than convicting a Mafia lieutenant of criminal charges and watching another take his place.

—STANLEY PENN

Carnival of Crime

AS Mardi Gras approaches, the Town and Country Motel near the airport in New Orleans likely will be booked solid, as will nearly all hotels and motels in the celebrating city.

A guest at the modern, 101-unit motel will find a convenient sight-seeing bus service, Southern Tours Inc., operating right from the Town and Country lobby. The $6 nightclub tour stops at such glittering burlesque palaces as the Sho-Bar on Bourbon Street. And perhaps someone at the motel will suggest dinner at the Elmwood Plantation Restaurant, a picturesque eating spot near the Levee.

In all this merrymaking, the tourist unwittingly will be patronizing a motel, tour service, nightclub and restaurant owned by close relatives of Carlos Marcello. They are just a few of the many seemingly legitimate businesses linked to Marcello, undisputed patriarch of the Cosa Nostra in Louisiana and the nearby Gulf Coast area.

Carlos ("The Little Man") Marcello is a short, pudgy 59-year-old Sicilian who has successfully resisted deportation, served time in Federal prison for marijuana peddling and now is appealing a two-year conviction for assaulting an FBI agent. He has repeatedly been identified as Cosa Nostra chief in the New Orleans area by experts testifying before Congressional committees.

But his notoriety hardly hampers him and his relatives and associates in playing a major role in business in Louisiana, along with the syndicate's more traditional interests in illegal gambling, narcotics, prostitution and other lucrative trades.

One of Marcello's key business interests is tourism, as is the case with many underworld groups. (In Florida, for example, the state has filed civil suits against 19 resort businesses in the Miami area alleged to be Mafia-controlled.) But Carlos Marcello is said to be the envy of other Mafia families because of the smooth, successful operations of his enterprises. "Marcello went further, sooner, than most other Mafia groups," says Ralph Salerno, former New York police investigator and now a consultant to the National Council on Crime and Delinquency.

The latest hint of Marcello's business maneuvers came when the chief of the Small Business Administration announced an investigation of an SBA loan to the Rowntowner Motor Inn in New Orleans because of suspected underworld connections. The SBA office in New Orleans guaranteed $288,750 of a construction loan for the $1.5 million motel, which is franchised by Downtowner Corp., a Memphis-based motel chain.

The Rowntowner's manager and 18% owner is Frank Occhipinti, a long-time business associate of the Marcellos and former owner, with a brother, Roy, of a motel in New Orleans franchised by Holiday Inns Inc. Holiday Inns forced the Occhipintis to sell the Holiday Inn motel after Senate testimony about the Occhipinti-Marcello connection. But the motel wound up in the hands of a group headed by Leon Poirier, a former Marcello accountant.

When Holiday Inns sought to cancel the franchise of the Poirier group, the owners sued Holiday Inns for $225 million. The suit was dropped after the Poirier group sold the motel to a Kansas operator, reportedly at a handsome profit.

The indications of Marcello's behind-the-scenes involvement in the motel business suggest to some observers that his visible influence on tourism is just the tip of the iceberg. Aaron Kohn, managing director of the Metropolitan Crime Commission of New Orleans, a private citizens' group that watches organized crime closely, says: "Tourism in New Orleans has become an invitation for people to come to the city to be paying guests of the Cosa Nostra."

Tourists each year pump $180 million into the New Orleans economy. The biggest day of the year is Mardi Gras—"Fat Tuesday." This is the day before Lent begins, when more than a million residents and out-of-towners jam the city in an orgy of drinking, parading and dancing. The Chamber of Commerce conservatively estimates spending during Carnival (the pre-Lenten festival that begins 12 days after Christmas and ends on Mardi Gras) at more than $11 million, including $500,-000 at bars and nightclubs on Mardi Gras alone.

There's no way to determine how much tourist spending finds its way into underworld hands, but a Dun & Bradstreet report nine years ago said, "It is thought that (Carlos Marcello) is the financial backer of at least 50% of the motels in the New Orleans area and Jefferson Parish area." Jefferson Parish adjoins New Orleans and is Marcello's home base.

Most of Marcello's suspected business interests are in other people's names. His Town and Country Motel, for example, was transferred to his three children in 1964. But a Dun & Bradstreet report two years later said, "Carlos Marcello is believed to be the real principal."

The Sho-Bar on Bourbon Street (featuring Ricki Covette, billed as "the world's tallest exotic" at six-feet-eight) is owned by Peter Marcello, one of Carlos' brothers and a close companion. Peter Marcello, who also owns or has owned other French Quarter clubs, spent time in Leavenworth for marijuana possession and has a long arrest record.

Another brother, Joseph Marcello Jr., is listed as an owner of the Elmwood Plantation Restaurant as well as the Holiday Motel (not related to Holiday Inns) in Jefferson Parish. Still another brother, Anthony, is a one-third owner of Southern Tours and once managed the Town and Country for brother Carlos, a job now held by one of Carlos' sons.

None of Mr. Marcello's alleged associates are more interesting at the moment than Frank and Roy Occhipinti. Their father was a friend of Carlos Marcello, and when the senior Occhipinti died in 1946, Carlos signed a bond so his widow could serve as administrator of the estate. Since then, the two sons—now in their early 40s—have found Marcello a valuable partner.

In the 1950s, they joined Marcello to build and jointly own the Town and Country Motel. In the 1964 maneuver, they disposed of it for an undisclosed consideration to Marcello's three children. "I completely sold my interest," says Frank Occhipinti.

In 1958, Frank and Roy incorporated Jacqueline Inc. to hold title to the Holiday Inn in New Orleans. Carlos Marcello's participation was suspected but never proven, according to Holiday Inn officials in Memphis. But in a U.S. Tax Court proceeding in 1969 involving the Marcello family, the court found that Carlos Marcello was beneficial owner of half of the Jacqueline stock nominally held by the Occhipintis.

Around 1968, Frank Occhipinti and seven partners formed La Strada Inn Inc., obtaining a Rowntowner franchise for their new 102-unit motel, restaurant and cocktail lounge. The other partners have no known association with Marcello and include three men in a well-known local accounting firm, Duplantier, Hrapmann & Hogan. One of these accountants, William R. Hogan Jr., says that the suspicions of a Mafia link with La Strada "are completely unfounded" and that none of the owners has ever had any underworld ties "except possibly Mr. Occhipinti at one time."

Frank Occhipinti angrily denies the Mafia charge. "Anyone who says this motel is dominated by the Mafia is crazy," he snaps. And he happily reports that "business is fantastic," with all signs pointing to a record Carnival season.

Mr. Kohn of the Crime Commission is among those who doubt that Frank and Roy Occhipinti have put their underworld associations behind them. Roy presently faces charges of possessing jewelry alleged to be part of an $80,000 burglary in Louisville in 1967. Frank remains a one-third owner of Southern Tours along with Carlos Marcello's brother Anthony and says he also has a one-third interest in Dixie Land Sight Seeing Tours Inc., also with Anthony Marcello as a partner. These two tour services have most of the business from motels along Airline and Chef Menteur highways, the major roads leading into the city from the east and west.

"The Occhipintis continue to be among the most important money movers of the Marcello organization," asserts Mr. Kohn. By this he means that they allegedly help invest the syndicate's huge revenues from illicit gambling and other activities in legitimate businesses, partly to help the mob explain its standard of living to Internal Revenue agents.

The public suspicions raised about the Rowntowner in New Orleans have caused Downtowner Corp. to launch its own investigation. R. L. Kirkpatrick, chairman and president, voices "deep concern" over the incident but adds that "inasmuch as La Strada and its principals strictly performed all of their obligations under their franchise contract," attorneys for Downtowner advised him "that the possible cancelation of the franchise agreement was questionable."

The Downtowner executive says the company made only "routine credit investigations" before granting the New Orleans franchise. "As a result of questions raised currently, (Downtowner) is deepening its investigatory functions to include resort to governmental and other agencies having access to information concerning the entire historical background of franchise applicants," he says.

Other popular tourist spots in New Orleans are in the hands of men linked to the New Orleans underworld. One is the 500 Club, a burlesque spot that ranks with the Sho-Bar as one of the largest and busiest on Bourbon Street. One of its owners is Frank Caracci. He is presently facing charges of attempting to bribe an Internal Revenue agent. He has pleaded innocent. Caracci also once owned the Court of Two Sisters, a famed French Quarter restaurant, and still owns the property on which it is located. According to the Crime Commission's Mr. Kohn Caracci is "closely affiliated" with Carlos Marcello.

"Tourists leave New Orleans seeing the part of the city that the Cosa Nostra wants them to see," says Mr. Kohn sadly.

—HERBERT G. LAWSON

Inside Jobs

THE worker looks like any other busy employe as he strides swiftly through the shadowy parking lot of a massive warehouse on New York City's West Side. Except for one thing: The bright violet hem of a woman's dress hanging below his jacket.

The worker is a thief. He steals from his employer, and he and his kind are giving American business a $4 billion headache. Employe theft has always been a problem for companies, but executives say that in recent years it has worsened. It is especially acute in consumer goods distribution and retailing, where large amounts of merchandise and sometimes cash pass through the hands of many workers.

The thieves are most often those directly involved with the flow of goods—sales clerks, stockroom employes, drivers of delivery trucks, warehousemen, cashiers. But in a surprising number of cases such workers are in collusion with their own supervisors or higher executives.

Few company officials like to talk about stealing by employes, but sources who know say it often accounts for three-fourths and sometimes more of all "inventory shrinkage"—an accounting euphemism for missing goods. Among many department stores and clothing retailers, such shortages have nearly doubled in recent years to 3% and sometimes 4% of sales.

"Maybe 90% of your employes have integrity, but the other 10% can devastate you," says Sanford Edelman, vice president in charge of thwarting employe theft at E. J. Korvette, a New York-based discount chain. Just whom the thief devastates is open to question, however. Most companies write off "inventory shrinkage" as an operating expense and slap the cost onto the consumer in the form of higher prices. Thus, a store that finds its employes are stealing goods valued at 3% of annual sales may simply raise its prices 3%— plus whatever more is necessary to cover the cost of attempts at theft prevention.

Surprisingly, the rising theft on the part of employes isn't accompanied by a rising sophistication in the techniques of stealing. Most workers resort to tactics no more deft than that of the warehouse worker who stuffs dresses under his coat and sneaks them out to his car. "I'd have to stop to think of anything really foxy," says Korvette's Mr. Edelman. "Most (theft) is pretty simple."

At a major Manhattan department store, sales clerks in the necktie department use several methods for stealing ties, according to a former employe. For women clerks, the simplest tactic is to stuff their purses with ties. Men stroll into restrooms, put the stolen tie on and wear it out of the store. Also, tie clerks may simply write each other "even-exchange" slips on ties they want to steal and then flash the slips at security guards when they leave the building openly carrying the stolen goods; such slips are supposed to indicate a previous purchase has been returned and exchanged for a different item of the same price.

But if the thieves lack cunning, so do some security men assigned to catch them. Bloomingdale's, a big New York-area department store, uses its own plainclothesmen to watch for shoplifting and employe theft. Supposedly, clerks can't spot the store detectives. "But you get to know who they are," says one ex-employe. "They dress like shoppers, but some of them are friends of the clerks and they'll come up, lean on the counter and chat. Once, a man who looked like a customer went behind my counter and picked up the phone. When I tried to stop him, he said: 'Shhh—I'm with Protection.' "

Although some inside thieves are replenishing their own wardrobes or decorating their homes, many sell their loot. Helen C., a price marker at a New York department store, recently confided to a fellow worker that she had stolen a $140 camera from the stockroom, and she offered to sell it to him for $50. The employe paid her a deposit and agreed to meet her at a nearby bar to close the deal. Unfortunately for Helen, the buyer turned out to be an undercover investigator, and as she made her "sale" two security officers closed in, took the camera and told Helen she was fired.

During the whole incident Helen remained unaware that the supposed "buyer" was a company investigator. So later that evening the man phoned her at home and asked for his money back. Not one to miss an opportunity, Helen invited him to her apartment, where she displayed five other cameras she had stolen from the store. Preserving his cover, the man declined to buy a camera, departed and later reported his findings to the store. The firm got the five cameras back, but it estimated that Helen had stolen and resold over $1,000 worth of merchandise before she was nabbed.

Most thieves steal in the assurance that if caught they will merely be fired, not prosecuted. Taking an employe to court for stealing creates what most companies consider bad publicity, and hauling one culprit after another before the bench and into the spotlight could do permanent damage, firms fear. "They're afraid the average customer will take his business elsewhere if he finds out that one out of every 10 or 20 employes steals and three cents is added to every dollar of price to pay for it," says one management consultant.

The warehouseman who steals dresses, for example, is being watched by his company, which wants to find out if he's acting alone or in collusion with others; as soon as that's determined, he'll be apprehended and fired. But company officials doubt they'll prosecute.

If an employe doesn't want to risk dealing with a fellow worker to dispose of stolen goods, middlemen willing to buy his loot abound. Saul D. Astor, president of Management Safeguards Inc., a private investigation firm, claims some bartenders in the central shopping district of Manhattan specialize in purchasing stolen goods. The bartenders often sell the merchandise to small retailers.

Investigators say uncovering employe theft is a relatively simple task. The real trick is to keep it under control once it's discovered. Consider the large baking company whose 39 route drivers for years routinely slipped up to 4,000 loaves of bread a day to supermarket managers in return for kickbacks. The company knew the problem existed—records of the drivers' loads seldom matched up with store receipts—but it chose to look the other way and write off the shortages as an operating expense.

But early in 1970 things came to a head. Because prices were already rising, it became more difficult to tack the cost of the thievery on to the retail price of the bread. Just as distressing was the company's inability to expand its routes; drivers were too busy servicing their under-the-counter accounts to take on new legitimate customers. So the company began charging the drivers the full wholesale price, an average of 29 cents per loaf, for bread unaccounted for. The firm said it made the move to "remove indifference among the drivers and create a sense of responsibility."

What it created was a sense of ingenuity. Drivers countered by continuing their illicit sales and replacing bread so disposed of—with day-old bread purchased for 10 cents a loaf from the company's own day-old bread store.

The company was initially exuberant when sales in its day-old bread stores shot up more than 20% in three months. Then it caught on, and began coding the bread wrappers, making substitution of day-old bread for missing loaves impossible.

The toughest theft rings to crack are those involving supervisors or executives, investigators say. "I'm not afraid Fred (a boss) will report me for stealing; I've seen him stealing many times," a sales clerk at one New York store told an undercover detective. In a different department of the same store, two stockroom supervisors were found to be actually recruiting and paying underlings to steal for them. Norman Jaspan, head of a New York investigation firm, says of the $75 million in fraud uncovered by his men last year, well over half was perpetrated by supervisors and higher company officials.

Store owners have found insurance policies against employe theft offer little comfort. Losses have soared so much in recent years that most firms can afford only high-deductible coverage. Underwriters say deductibles of $50,000 to $100,000 per theft aren't uncommon. Since few thefts are of that magnitude, companies seldom collect. Most recover less than 15% of their theft losses from insurance.

When asked why employes steal so often and so

much, most company officials echo the opinion of Sol W. Cantor, chairman of Interstate Department Stores, who blames "declining morality in American society." Maybe so, investigators say, but dishonesty is mostly a product of being offered the chance to be dishonest. Most companies, they contend, are robbed by employes because of sloppy supervision and a failure to enforce rules already laid down.

Few firms, for example, give new employes the thorough screening that official policy usually calls for, say the consultants who are called in once employe theft begins to reach unmanageable proportions. Out of 14 employes who were recently fired from one discount store for thievery, eight strolled across the parking lot and got jobs in a supermarket in the same shopping center, says an executive of the discounter.

To stop just that sort of thing, department stores in many cities have formed "mutual protective associations" in which they trade names of former workers who have been bounced for theft and watch for these names when screening job applicants.

Korvette's parent corporation, Spartans Industries, has adopted this idea on a broader scale by forming a new subsidiary, Stores Prevent Inc. The operation keeps a computer "bank" of names, birth dates, Social Security numbers and other data on all former Spartans employes dismissed for stealing. The company offers the service to other firms nationwide and asks them to submit similar information for the computer on their own bad apples.

—DAVID MCCLINTICK

Whirr, Click—Eureka!

"**I** COULD steal a company blind in three months and leave its books looking balanced," boasts Sheldon Dansiger, a burly, 33-year-old data-processing specialist.

His method: Electronic embezzlement. His accomplice: The company's own computer.

Increasingly, business transactions that formerly were recorded on ledger pages are being translated into magnetic impulses in a computer's memory section. It's a simple matter for a crook with technical know-how and a little imagination to program a computer to fleece a company and fool its auditors, according to Mr. Dansiger.

He says corporate executives rarely question the reliability of financial results that emerge from complex million-dollar machines. "They simply forget that the machines have been built to do whatever the operators direct," explains Mr. Dansiger. "There's nothing to stop them from working quite efficiently for a crook."

Joseph J. Wasserman, who heads a Bell Telephone Laboratories task force seeking to devise methods of auditing computers used by the Bell System, says many companies already have been hit with heavy losses, but their managements don't know it. He predicts that within a few years someone will uncover a computerized embezzlement that will make even the $150 million salad oil swindle seem puny.

Computers are operating faster and faster and producing fewer and fewer of the printouts that auditors and financial officers need to follow the flow of dollars processed by the machines. "If auditing staffs don't get involved in designing computer systems soon, they might just as well climb up on their stools, pull down their green eyeshades and pray for retirement to come," says Mr. Wasserman.

Others who are aware of the growing problem echo the sentiments of Messrs. Dansiger and Wasserman. "If I were a crook, I'd work through computers," asserts Robert Fano, a leading computer theoretician at Massachusetts Institute of Technology. Ralph Salerno, a former New York City detective who is now a member of a state committee investigating organized crime in New York, says: "I'm not a gambling man, but if I were, I'd bet a month's pay that the Mafia will be working with computers in a few years."

A number of electronic embezzlements already have come to light. The manager in charge of back-office operations at Walston & Co., a New York brokerage firm, electronically siphoned $250,000 out of the company between 1951 and 1959. By the time the theft was uncovered, the man had become a vice president.

He programed Walston's computer to transfer money from a company account to two customers' accounts—his and his wife's. The computer was further programed to show the money had gone to purchase stock for the two accounts. Then he sold the stock supposedly purchased, pocketed the cash and transferred some more.

When a Walston official sensed something was amiss, an examination of the two accounts revealed major irregularities. But the company couldn't figure out the embezzler's system. Because he hadn't stolen any money from customers' accounts, "what he did was absolutely undetectable without internal auditing," says William D. Fleming, Walston president. "Before it happened no one dreamed such a thing was possible, and if he hadn't explained how he did it, we probably still wouldn't know."

The thief explained to Walston's incredulous directors that he pulled off the elaborate money swap by going into the office early Sunday mornings to punch new computer cards and feed them into the machines. "It took someone with absolute knowledge of the computer system to do it," says Mr. Fleming. "This guy was the boss back there. He set up the system and ran the whole show."

Walston recovered only a fraction of the stolen money. The firm promptly revamped its computer system, instituting a quarterly internal audit and other safeguards designed to foil embezzlement attempts. The former vice president served a year in Sing Sing prison and is now a furniture salesman.

Even as the Walston theft was being uncovered, a similar embezzlement was beginning at another New York brokerage firm, Carlisle & Jacquelin. From 1959 to 1963, the firm's data-processing manager got away with $81,120 by instructing a computer to write checks to fictitious persons and send them to his home address. The scheme was uncovered when the Post Office accidently returned one of the checks to the firm and the clerk who received it became suspicious.

George Muller, a manager partner of Carlisle & Jacquelin, refuses to discuss the case. "We'd have to be crazy to give out all the details now so that anyone who wanted to could do it again," says Mr. Muller. Court records show that the embezzler was convicted, returned the money and received a suspended sentence.

More recently, National City Bank of Minneapolis discovered that the employe who programed the computerized check-handling system it set up in 1965 embezzled $1,357 over a period of about a year. He programed the computer to completely disregard his personal checks any time his account had insufficient funds to cover them. The computer allowed each of his bad checks to clear the bank and didn't debit the employe's account for the overdrafts.

The scheme was discovered only by accident, when a computer breakdown forced hand-processing of some checks. One of the embezzler's bad checks bounced. When bank officials confronted him, the employe readily disclosed his scheme. The ex-employe later pleaded guilty, repaid the money and received a suspended sentence.

Computer specialists tell of other ways employes can program computers to steal for them. A crook can change one figure in a computer program, and the machine will report abnormally high inventory losses as normal merchandise breakage, enabling accomplices to steal vast amounts of goods from warehouses without the theft being noticed. Later the operator can remove the evidence simply by putting the original figure back into the computer program.

Computerized payroll systems are potential bonanzas for embezzlers, the experts say. A computer operator can create paychecks for fictitious employes and pay extra overtime and wages to himself quite simply. If he's more ambitious, he can program the computer to deduct a few extra pennies of "income tax" from every paycheck in the plant and pay himself the amount collected.

It's possible to program some safeguards against embezzlement into computers, the specialists say, but the process is complicated and costly and sometimes involves entirely rewriting computer programs and shutting down the machines for a time. Adding safeguards "will cost a company money, and the temptation is often to economize," says Roy Freed, counsel for the computer control division of Honeywell Inc.

But even the most elaborate safeguards might not foil a skilled embezzler. There's always the danger that a crook will come along who's more clever than the specialists who programed the safeguards into the computer. Lloyd McChesney, chief examiner for the New York Stock Exchange, says that although member firms recently tightened their computer auditing procedures, "no one has yet developed a way to keep his books with a 100% guarantee against embezzlements."

Data-processing specialists, however, say there are a few basic rules company officials can follow at least to make it more difficult for a computer crook to raid the corporate treasury.

A cardinal rule, according to the specialists: Don't let the computer programer actually operate the machine. A crook who can build a loophole into the system and also feed it the data necessary to carry out his embezzlement scheme is more likely to succeed than a crook who, after programing the machine, must sit back and hope another operator will innocently let the machine divert funds to him.

Manuel Stonewood—who, with Mr. Dansiger, operates a New York management consulting and "computer sleuthing" firm called EDP Associates Inc.—says he passed up some golden opportunities to steal large sums from a major New York City bank not long ago. "I also designed a mutual fund's dividend payment system for the bank, wrote the program for it, then ran the job on the computer," says Mr. Stonewood.

"The operation was so big it had a mistake tolerance of several hundred thousand dollars," claims Mr. Stonewood. "I could have paid at least half that much to myself in small checks if I had been so inclined, and the money wouldn't have been missed."

A second rule recommended by the specialists: Segregate computerized check-writing operations from the departments that authorize checks. This setup makes it difficult for an embezzler to convert fudged data into actual cash pay-outs. And it makes it easier for management to spot checks issued by a computer that has been tampered with.

Another rule: Transfer computer programers and operators frequently to different machines and different programs. The theory is that if a crook knows he won't be working on a single job long enough to bilk it for large sums, he's less likely to go to the trouble of rigging the computer to steal. Even if he does rig it, the next man on that job may spot the embezzlement procedure.

What such safeguards fail to prevent, auditors are supposed to catch, of course. But many data-processing specialists say most auditors don't understand computers, so a clever embezzler can fool them. Some large accounting firms have developed their own highly skilled staffs of computer auditors, but even these specialists can be deceived because so much of what goes on inside the machine never appears on a computer print-out.

"Unless you build right into the system a means of printing out audit information, you aren't going to get readable financial records anymore," says Mr. Wasserman of Bell Labs. He says his team of specialists already has developed several new computer auditing techniques that might eventually be used throughout the Bell System.

One technique involves programing a computer to spot seeming irregularities in operating procedures and immediately print out a copy of the questionable transaction for auditors to examine. Another method entails feeding test data into a computer and then checking to determine whether anything interfered with proper processing.

Mr. Wasserman says the Bell System's auditing setup will do far more than spot crooks. For one thing, it will alert executives more quickly to fluctuations in overtime costs, inventory changes and other areas that can have an immediate impact on corporate profits. He says computers currently are used to check the efficiency of telephone operators and to audit employes' calls to guard against widespread misuse of long-distance equipment.

—ALAN ADELSON

Underworld Genius

THE attorney general of Florida is investigating the affairs of Meyer Lansky, possibly the most powerful leader of organized crime in the country.

Does that bother Meyer Lansky? Sure it does. It bothers him about as much as the FBI agents who tail him constantly—the agents who have discovered that whenever their car starts to fall behind, Meyer Lansky's car slows down to let them catch up.

That's the way it is in the world of Meyer Lansky —a man who for 50 years has thwarted the best efforts of Federal, state and local lawmen to put him behind bars for good and who can't really be expected to stay awake nights just because one more cop has joined the parade. But Meyer Lansky, now 67, has done more than remain free. He has remained a power—some say *the* power—in the underworld. Indeed, of the group that in the 1930s founded the giant conglomerate that is organized crime today, Lansky alone survives and wields power. And that, perhaps, is more a measure of the man.

So it's not surprising that on a recent sunny Friday afternoon, while both Attorney General Earl Faircloth and Governor Claude Kirk were threatening vigorous campaigns against organized crime in Florida, Lansky was coolly walking his dog in front of the luxury apartment building where he lives, his countenance as cheerful as the blue-checkered shirt he wore. Only when a car slowed alongside did apprehension cross his face, and he dashed into his beachfront apartment at 5001 Collins Avenue, just up the road from the Fontainebleau Hotel.

Notoriety may be the only thing Meyer Lansky fears. Guided by that fear and by a mind that is easily the most brilliant in the underworld, he has shaped the organized crime syndicate into a well-disciplined operation. The syndicate as ruled by Lansky and colleagues draws up contracts for mergers rather than murders and employs battalions of accountants and attorneys, not bodyguards.

"If Meyer Lansky had gone into legitimate business instead of into the mob back in the 1920s, he'd be the chairman of the board of General Motors today," says a Federal agent with grudging admiration. It was Lansky who persuaded the syndicate to de-emphasize such high-risk and high-publicity ventures as narcotics, prostitution and murder-by-contract and to plunge into the safer, more profitable fields of banking, insurance, real estate and gambling, both legal and illegal. And it was Lansky who pioneered in developing the intricate network of fronts that allows the syndicate to operate numerous enterprises without revealing a visible connection to them.

That system works like this: Mob money is sent to numbered bank accounts in Switzerland via courier. Middlemen in Europe then draw out some of the money and send it to agents—usually lawyers or brokers—in the U.S., sometimes with specific instructions on how to invest it, sometimes with orders to invest it in any manner the agent sees fit. The middleman in Europe knows who he's working for. The agent who deals with the middleman usually doesn't.

Federal agents estimate Lansky's personal fortune in numbered accounts abroad may approach $300 million. Lately, a lot of that money has been finding its way back to the U.S. to be invested in real estate in Florida and the Caribbean. (In such transfers of Lansky money, the key middleman is often John Pullman, a Russian-born Canadian now living in Switzerland.)

Lansky has been known to put money directly into businesses, too—when he's sure he has a front man whose lips are sealed. Attorney General Faircloth has charged that Lansky and other racketeers are behind many of Miami Beach's plush motels. He recently filed 21 civil suits against 15 motels under a controversial new state law that gives him the power to revoke the corporate charters of any firm directly or indirectly connected to organized crime.

But there's some doubt about the new law's Constitutionality—to say nothing of the likelihood of getting hard proof of a connection between the motels and mob figures like Lansky. "Even if the law sticks, all Lansky and his pals have to do is replace old front men with new ones and they're back in business," says one skeptical investigator who has pursued mobsters for years.

Adds another law enforcement agent: "It's going to take more than a few civil suits to touch a man like Meyer Lansky."

What manner of man is Lansky? The standard Hollywood portrait of an underworld king-pin is well-known. He should be paunchy, in keeping with a love for good food and wine. He should have diamonds and sapphires sparkling on his pudgy fingers. His suits should be as flashy as the showgirls on his arm. He should have a loud, jovial manner that can turn suddenly to murderous rage when he is crossed. He should live well and show it, luxuriating in penthouse apartments, country estates and black limousines.

Meyer Lansky fits none of those stereotypes. He is a thin, gray-haired man with a pinched face, who wears conservative, modestly priced suits and speaks softly and with a wry sense of humor. Earlier this year a reporter asked him for a statement after a grand jury appearance. "I don't want to take the drama out of your stories, so I don't think I'll say anything," Lansky said as he walked away, smiling. Just before another grand jury appearance, Lansky joked with reporters who requested interviews and gave a bit of fatherly Jewish advice: "If you don't have a sense of humor, you don't have anything."

As befits one so mild of manner, Lansky lives in a style that would provoke no jealousy in any upper-middle-class neighborhood. Until recently, he lived in a $60,000 ranch-house in Hallendale, a Miami suburb, and drove a rented Chevrolet. He sold the house and moved into a beachfront apartment with tighter security after he began to fear that "young Turks" of the underworld might try to kidnap him for ransom—a fate that befell some New York gang leaders last year.

Lansky's "office" is a backroom in the Singapore Hotel in Miami Beach, where he meets friends and colleagues and conducts "business." He is said to spend much of his time thinking up and implementing new projects and prefers to let his lieutenants run his established enterprises. He takes frequent trips to Europe—ostensibly for pleasure, in fact for both pleasure and business.

In trying to foster the image of a genial, withdrawn businessman of modest means, Lansky is thorough to the last detail. It's said that in filing his income tax returns, he portrays himself as a retired investor living in moderate comfort off the return of a few prudent holdings. He is reported to justify every expenditure to the last cent and even to skip some of the deductions he is entitled to.

Partly to preserve the image, partly because he *does* value his privacy, Lansky doesn't like to be crowded—by either the law or his colleagues. When he feels that's happening, he resorts to a favorite trick to throw off those who hound him—he pretends he is a sick man, close to death.

Whenever the heat is on—an investigation made public, a grand jury inquiry, a new task force of Federal crimefighters on his trail—stories suddenly abound that Meyer Lansky is dying of cancer or has some other terminal illness. In the files of the New York State Police, there exists a report made out in the 1920s that says Meyer Lansky is a bad guy, all right, but there's no need to worry because he's a sickly man who won't live out the year. In fact, Lansky looks 10 years younger than his age and enjoys excellent health. "He'll probably live to be 100," says an old friend and former racketeer.

It is because Lansky doesn't fit the flamboyant picture of the crime boss that he is still around, lawmen say. Those of his early colleagues who savored the sweet life—Bugsy Siegel, Frank Costello, Louis Lepke, Lucky Luciano—have paid dearly for enjoying the spotlight of center stage; all of them have been either murdered, knocked from power, imprisoned or deported. Fellow gangsters deposed Frank Costello, for example, because he had become too much of an attention-attracting personality. Bugsy Siegel was machine-gunned to death after his lavish spending got him into hock with gang chieftains.

But despite the inconspicuous manner, Meyer Lansky is no stranger to the violence and strong-arm tactics of the underworld. Born Maier Suchowjansky in Grodno, Russia, Lansky arrived in the U.S. at age nine. His family settled in New York's immigrant slums. By the time he was 27, young Maier had five arrests on his record, on charges ranging from disorderly conduct to suspicion of murder, but he was never convicted. He had begun his painstaking climb up the underworld ladder.

In 1926, a man named John Barrett was found in a New York alley, near death from bullet wounds. At the hospital, Barrett said Lansky had shot him after an argument over the division of loot from a warehouse robbery, and he agreed to testify to that effect in court. A few days later, Barrett's hospital food was somehow poisoned. He recovered, but he got the message and refused to sign a complaint.

It was during the 1920s that Lansky became a pal and partner of Bugsy Siegel. The two became a formidable pair, first as hired gunmen for Legs Diamond, soon as leaders of their own gang, called the "Bugs and Meyer Mob." Their specialty was protecting liquor in transit from hijackers to East Coast gangs. They were good at it, and when an alliance called the Eastern syndicate was formed to coordinate rum-running, Lansky and Siegel were named to the board. Lansky was put in charge of handling the syndicate's finances.

By the early 1930s, the Eastern syndicate began to form a loose alliance with other regional mobs. Thus was the national syndicate born. Each gang retained its own identity and pursued its own activities, with the federation coming together occasionally to discuss matters of common interest. Final decisions rested with individual gang leaders, with one acting as federation chairman. The first chairman was Lucky Luciano, head of the Mafia in the East.

In the federation, Lansky and his New York cohorts learned that some gangs relied on more subtle methods. The Cleveland syndicate, for example, preferred the bribe to the bullet, and its leaders led quiet personal lives, careful to provide themselves with convincing fronts. Lansky began to ponder their methods.

But during the 1930s, there was little time for reflection. With the repeal of prohibition, activities such as prostitution, hijacking, gambling, narcotics and extortion became more important to the mob. Lansky, Siegel, Luciano and Lepke set up a factory to process drugs. Lepke founded a group of paid killers who replaced the Bugs and Meyer Mob and became the syndicate's enforcement arm. The group was dubbed Murder Incorporated and killed over 800 persons before racketbusters Burton Turkus and Thomas E. Dewey put it out of business and sent Lepke to the electric chair.

The efforts of the two prosecutors shook the Eastern syndicate to its roots. Siegel fled to Hollywood. Lansky found New York too hot for comfort and moved to Florida. Luciano stood his ground and lost—he was convicted by Mr. Dewey and sentenced to 50 years in prison. But 1,200 miles to the south, Meyer Lansky was finding Florida to be fertile ground. Remembering the lessons of the Cleveland syndicate, he sowed bribes among police and politicians and his efforts bore fruit.

Many years later the Kefauver Committee heard Walter Clark, sheriff of Broward County, Fla., confess that from 1933 to 1952 he provided "special policing" for Lansky's illegal gambling houses and even deputized the Lansky men who carried the cash in armored cars from the casinos to banks.

During World War II, Lansky played a part in an incredible alliance between the underworld and the U.S. Navy. The full story has never been told, although some clues came out in the Kefauver hearings a decade later. Apparently, the Navy decided East Coast piers could be protected from sabotage only with the aid of the Mafia. Lucky Luciano was locked away, but he still held power and the loyalty of Mafia members. Luciano's attorney and Meyer Lansky were recruited to persuade Luciano to give the arrangement his blessing. After several months of prison visits, Luciano agreed—to exactly what, it isn't known, but after the war, Lucky was paroled and sent home to Italy on promise he would never again enter the U.S.

With Luciano gone, a triumvirate of Lansky, Joe Adonis and Frank Costello took over leadership of the syndicate. By the late 1950s, Costello had been ousted from power by his colleagues and Adonis had been deported. Lansky sat alone at the top. Meantime, his old friends still on lower rungs of the ladder began to fall by the wayside. Bugsy Siegel poured so much mob money into the building of the Flamingo Hotel in Las Vegas that, when it promptly flopped upon opening, he was gunned down.

That crime was never solved, but over the years Lansky has shown a continuing keen interest in the fortunes of the Flamingo. In 1960, when the owner of the hotel-casino—Parvin-Dohrmann Co. of Los Angeles—began casting about for a buyer, Lansky turned up again. The company paid him $200,000 as a "finders fee" to help sell the hotel to a group headed by Morris Landsburgh, a Florida hotel man.

A contract signed by Lansky and Albert Parvin, then head of the company, reads: "Flamingo recognizes and acknowledges that it has been solely through the information and advice supplied by Lansky that the sale may be made. . . ." (Asked recently how he came to secure Lansky's aid, Mr. Parvin said, "I'm not going to talk to you. I don't know what you're talking about. You press people never print the truth anyway. You're not getting any answer from me.")

Between Bugsy Siegel's death in 1947 and the 1960 sale of the Flamingo, Lansky kept busy, expanding his power and the scope of the mob's operations. He also discovered a new romance. A pretty manicurist at New York's Embassy Hotel named Thelma Schwartz so captivated him that he obtained a divorce from his wife, Anna, along with custody of his three children. (Such was Lansky's power that he secured a West Point appointment for his eldest son, who did well at the academy and rose to the rank of captain before leaving the Army.)

In the postwar boom, Lansky's enterprise flourished as well as his family life. He set up real estate companies and jukebox distribution outlets in several states, along with a new chain of illegal and highly lucrative casinos. With the foresight of a Wall Street expert, he even put syndicate money into the new fields of television set distribution and servicing. Although young hoods today are still much taken with the reputation Lansky built in the 1920s as a cool and efficent killer, it is his later business acumen that has won him universal respect in the underworld. Anyone who has associated with Meyer Lansky has made money; thus his friendship, attention and approval are zealously sought.

The only hiatus in the Lansky career occurred in 1950 when the Kefauver Committee turned its attention to him, giving the world the first hint of his vast power.

That setback was only minor. Lansky was forced to shut down his casinos in Florida and New York and was indicted for gambling violations. But efforts to deport him failed, and the worst that befell him was a three-month jail sentence. After his release, Lansky found new ground for profits in Cuba, a short hop from his Miami base. He persuaded Fulgencio Batista, then in power, to pass a law that said gambling was allowed only in hotels worth over $1 million and then proceeded to build the only hotels that qualified. That happy state of affairs lasted until Fidel Castro came to power in 1959—Batista and Lansky fled Cuba on the same day.

Although still busy involving the syndicate in real estate and other legitimate businesses in the U.S., Lansky kept an eye out for a Caribbean venture to replace his monopoly in Cuba. When gambling was legalized in the Bahamas, and a new casino opened at the Lucayan Beach Hotel, several Lansky associates were found to be in charge. Then in 1966 revelations of questionable payments to government officials toppled the United Bahamian Party from power, and Lansky's associates were expelled from the Bahamas by the new government. (Fear of Lansky's influence remains strong in the Bahamas; when Hyman Lazar, one of the Lucayan Beach casino's new managers was observed fraternizing with Lansky in Miami Beach recently, the present owners of the casino quickly booted him out.)

The setback in the Bahamas didn't curtail Lansky's interest in gambling. Federal officials believe he has extensive holdings in casinos in England, southern Europe and the Middle East, and no one is yet dismissing the likelihood that Lansky money is still, in some way, present and growing in Las Vegas. But what undoubtedly really cheers Meyer Lansky is the growing movement to legalize gambling in his own backyard—Miami Beach.

Hotel owners in the area are feverishly backing the movement because they're convinced they are losing business to the hotel-casinos in Puerto Rico and the Bahamas. Several Florida politicians, with one eye on the financial backing hotel owners can supply them, have come out in favor of a referendum to permit casinos in Miami Beach. Even Gov. Kirk—he of the vows to wage relentless war on organized crime in Florida—felt compelled to tell an audience recently that there is a difference between casinos controlled by the syndicate and those operated by up-and-up businessmen. "Don't tar all casinos with the same brush," cautioned the governor.

So it's no wonder that Meyer Lansky continues to foster the image of an up-and-up businessman. And with new opportunities opening up every day and old enterprises flourishing, it's no wonder Meyer Lansky looked the perfect picture of a happy man on that recent bright Friday afternoon as he walked his dog on the sun-drenched streets of Miami Beach.

—NICHOLAS GAGE

Wolfson's World

IF Louis Wolfson is to be believed, he could have obtained a Presidential pardon in December 1968, sparing him the anguish of a one-year jail sentence that faces him for the illegal sale of stock.

Through political connections, the millionaire industrialist says, he could have secured a pardon from President Johnson if he had asked for it. Wolfson says he received this assurance "from somebody who is as close as anybody could be" to Mr. Johnson.

The industrialist says he turned down the opportunity because he didn't want any favors.

Wolfson was interviewed in his ranch-style home in Miami Beach where he is putting his affairs in order. He is expected to surrender shortly to a U.S. marshal to serve a jail term at a Federal prison at Eglin Air Force Base near Pensacola, Fla.

In jail, Wolfson plans to read and work. "I'll do anything the others are doing," he says. "I don't want any special treatment whatsoever."

At the height of his success, Wolfson was chairman and controlling stockholder of an industrial empire whose sales reached $436 million in 1959.

Under his direction, Merritt-Chapman & Scott Corp., a construction company, became one of the first of the large conglomerates—expanding into shipbuilding, paint manufacture, chemicals and money lending.

In one year, Wolfson's pay and expenses from Merritt-Chapman reached $525,000.

Wolfson became a nationally prominent figure in 1955 when he mounted an unsuccessful proxy fight to win control of what was then Montgomery Ward & Co. from the late Sewell Avery, who was head of the big retailing company at the time.

Today, Wolfson's world is in pieces. Merritt-Chapman is in liquidation, and he has resigned as chairman. In 1966, Wolfson had a heart attack. His wife died of cancer in December 1968. At age 57, Wolfson is a husky six-footer, with a sun-tanned face. But his hair is graying, and some of the old robustness has left him.

Federal juries in New York in 1967 and 1968 convicted Wolfson on criminal charges growing out of stock transactions. A one-year sentence and a $100,000 fine were imposed on him for illegally selling unregistered stock in Continental Enterprises Inc., a Jacksonville, Fla., company in which he was a controlling shareholder.

Wolfson also faces an 18-month sentence and $32,-000 fine as a result of his conviction in 1968 in a case involving Merritt-Chapman. Wolfson, who is appealing that case, was convicted of perjury and conspiracy to obstruct justice in an investigation by the Securities and Exchange Commission, and for filing false and misleading company reports with the SEC.

Wolfson says his wealth has "declined substantially" in the last 10 years. Court fees, settlements of stockholder suits and reduction of income—these alone have cost $2.5 million to $5 million, he estimates.

But Wolfson, an immigrant junk dealer's son who founded his fortune on a borrowed $10,000, still has millions of dollars in holdings.

He says he has 425,000 shares, or more than 20%, of

Merritt-Chapman's stock outstanding. Wolfson, members of his family and associates own about 36% of the stock of Universal Marion Corp., a small Jacksonville movie and television production concern whose executive vice president is Wolfson's 28-year-old son Steven.

Wolfson still owns Harbor View Farm, near Ocala, Fla., one of the largest breeders of thoroughbred horses in the U.S. The payroll on this establishment alone amounts to $750,000 a year.

Among Universal Marion's interests is an 80% holding, acquired in June 1968, in the Miami Beach Sun, a small daily newspaper that has been building circulation with a continuing attack on crime.

Wolfson's conviction in the Continental case was hailed as a major victory for SEC investigators and for Robert M. Morgenthau, U.S. attorney for New York's southern district. These Federal officials have been cracking down hard in recent years on stock traders who violate securities laws.

Wolfson was among the first to be charged in a criminal action with violation of the section of the securities act that prohibits the sale of stock by a controlling stockholder unless the shares are first registered with the SEC. A registration statement provides vital information about the financial condition of a company. It is intended to permit the investor to buy and sell stock in a concern intelligently.

Government prosecutors charged that while Wolfson was selling his unregistered Continental stock, the price of the stock was being pushed up by release of favorable publicity about an aerosol-dispensing device the company licensed.

Wolfson claims he wasn't aware that he was violating SEC laws. He says his financial advisers told him the sale of the stock was legitimate. "I didn't use any fictitious names in selling the stock. No Swiss banks. When I made the sale I reported it to the SEC. I'd have had to be an idiot to do anything willfully wrong."

Wolfson maintains he has been made a scapegoat by the SEC. In his view, he was hit with criminal charges for the same kind of violations for which some officials of brokerage firms were penalized merely with fines and suspensions.

"No industrialist in America has been investigated by as many investigative committees as I have," Wolfson angrily says. This has soured him on the world of business and finance. After he gets out of jail, he says, "I never will be an officer, or a director of any publicly held company for the balance of my life."

Wolfson is disenchanted with Wall Street. He says he has seen greed and business immorality in the securities field. "You've got more crooks in Wall Street than in any other industry I've ever seen," he maintains.

Example: "I don't think it's right for a partner of a brokerage firm calling me up, saying I should sell a certain stock, while another partner urges another customer to buy that same stock. Basically, there is something dishonest about that. Either the stock is good or not."

Example: "Look at these investment bankers with seats on the boards of various corporations. These bankers, or their customers, trade in the stocks of those companies based on inside information." They have an advantage in buying and selling stock denied to the public, Wolfson says.

Example: "I've never seen so many underwriters coming out with stock issues that are just junk. It's a public disgrace. They have a moral obligation not to sell those."

Merritt-Chapman's collapse was a bitter pill for

Wolfson. He blames the collapse on blundering subordinates. Major decisions that led to huge losses were often based on misinformation and half-facts, he says.

"I remember a $7.3 million job we had," he says. "We estimated we would make a profit of $1.1 million. Instead we took a loss of $4.8 million. We had many more like that. There was such stupidity. People were drunk (on the job). There were (immoral) women on the job," Wolfson shakes his head in disgust.

Merritt-Chapman's failure was also brought on by severe losses at its New York Shipbuilding subsidiary, which got into arguments with the Navy, its chief customer, over the speed and quality of its operations. In 1967, the Navy terminated its last contract with the company.

Merritt-Chapman in 1960 was indicted by a Washington State grand jury on bribery charges in connection with the construction of a big dam on the Columbia River. It was charged that the company made gifts of cash, vacation trips and sterling silver to an official of the public utility district that backed the project. Merritt-Chapman pleaded no contest to six counts, and the other three counts were dismissed.

If Wolfson had it to do over again, he says, he would never try to capture control of Montgomery Ward, which merged in 1968 with Container Corp. of America to form Marcor Inc. He had sought the retailing company, in part, to tap its $300 million in cash and liquid assets for other corporate acquisitions. For the move, he was called a "corporate raider," a term he could never shake off. "People began to wonder where I was going to strike next," he says.

Wolfson previously had made enemies when, in 1949, he bought control of Capital Transit Co., a bus and street-car system in Washington, D.C. The company had accumulated a healthy cash surplus during the war years and for a period of time under Wolfson it paid out larger dividends than it was earning per share. But then Capital Transit's demands for a fare increase provoked a Congressional investigation, Wolfson was forced to sell the company.

Wolfson regrets he didn't quit Merritt-Chapman to take an active role in the management of American Motors Corp. when he was the auto company's biggest shareholder in 1958. He asserts he spent considerable time in helping George Romney, then head of American Motors, in reviving the auto manufacturer. At the time, two Wolfson representatives were on American Motors' board.

"I wanted to move into American Motors—as president or chairman—and make it my life's work," he says. Why then did he sell his American Motors stock? He says his colleagues at Merritt-Chapman begged him to get out. "It was taking too much of my time away from Merritt-Chapman. I yielded to their persuasion against my better judgment."

Alexander Rittmaster was a trusted colleague who, Wolfson said, advised him to get out of the auto concern. If Wolfson hates anybody, it is Mr. Rittmaster. A defendant in the Merritt-Chapman trial, Mr. Rittmaster was the chief Government witness against Wolfson. A prosecutor in that case said that without Mr. Rittmaster's testimony, Wolfson couldn't have been convicted. Mr. Rittmaster, who received $1.2 million in pay and fees from Merritt-Chapman over a 17-year period, got a four-month jail sentence after pleading guilty to a conspiracy charge.

Wolfson blames Mr. Rittmaster for his troubles with the SEC in connection with American Motors. Wolfson charges that Mr. Rittmaster, without any authorization, in 1958 publicly said that Wolfson was selling his American Motors stock. In fact, the stock had already been sold, and Wolfson was in a short position. That meant he had sold stock he had borrowed in the expectation that he could purchase replacement shares later at a lower price in the open market.

After the SEC went to court, Wolfson, while denying charges of wrongdoing, agreed to a permanent injunction against issuing any "false and misleading" statements about his holdings in American Motors or engaging in transactions that might "operate a fraud or deceit" on traders of those shares.

It may amuse Wolfson's enemies that he goes to his youth to cite examples of his own ethical misbehavior.

Wolfson was a great high school football player in Jacksonville. Many colleges sought him out when he graduated during the depression. Wolfson recalls that he demanded and got $100 a month in spending money to play for the University of Georgia. Other players on the team were getting $5 a month. Wolfson regrets now that he sought special treatment.

Wolfson also relates that when he was 15 or 16 he boxed professionally under the name of "Kid Wolf." He received $25 to $100 a bout. Wolfson says that since he was a professional prize fighter, he shouldn't have played high school football. That is another of his regrets.

—STANLEY PENN

King, Philosopher—and Thief

SAMMY Amalu sometimes calls himself a penologist —an expert on prison management. But he prefers the title Grand Thief. "There is something rather distinguished sounding in the appellation Grand Thief," he says. "Sounds a bit like Grand Mufti or Grand Chamberlain."

Sammy qualifies on either count. He has been in and out of prisons for much of his 50 years and currently resides in Folsom Prison in California, his home for the past six years. Sammy, however, is not your run-of-the-mill convict.

For one thing, he claims he is descended from Hawaiian royalty and refers to himself as His Highness Samuel Crowningburg-Amalu. For another, he may be the only newspaper columnist in the country who is behind bars. Writing from his cell in Folsom, Sammy three or four times a week analyzes the world with irreverent and sometimes Olympian rhetoric for the morning Honolulu Advertiser.

Sammy's readers are advised over their morning coffee of the plight of Hawaii's U.S. Senator Daniel Inouye: "He is intelligent and therefore must feel an overwhelming loneliness in Washington. Or in Honolulu for that matter." Attacking Vice President Agnew's "hop, step and a jump" tour of the Far East one winter,

Sammy told his readers: "I loathe instant coffee, abhor instant tea and utterly detest instant rice. . . . Yet I should far rather feast on such drab fare than sip the preposterous drivel of the instant expert."

Sammy, says Buck Buchwach, managing editor of the Advertiser, is "a bald-headed rebel who chides the Establishment in a genteel way." The paper itself refers to Sammy as "Our Pen Pal" or "widely respected con man." Thurston Twigg-Smith, the Advertiser's publisher, and an old high school chum of Sammy's, compares him to a comic strip character who never grows up.

Sammy started the column after four years of sitting in Folsom Prison corresponding with his old friend, Mr. Twigg-Smith. For a "Grand Thief," Sammy's crime seems a bit mundane: He was imprisoned for writing a $200 bum check, (Sammy's earlier stints in Leavenworth Prison and a Philippine prison were for the same crime). But that check was the crowning touch to a 1962 escapade that captured newspaper headlines around the world.

What was initially heralded by the Honolulu Advertiser as "perhaps the biggest deal of its kind in Hawaii history," turned out to be a hoax perpetrated by a penniless Sammy. He invented a mythical Swiss syndicate called International Trade Exchange that reached "agreement" to buy Sheraton Corp. of America's four Honolulu hotels for $34 million. Sheraton, which supposedly would have continued to operate the hotels under lease, had bought them only three years before—for only $18 million. The "syndicate" also made offers for other Hawaii properties for a total package of $62 million.

Sammy, his exploits already well known in Hawaii, stayed in the background; even his front men, includ-

ing a surfer he had picked up at the airport and granted the title "Pro-Regent" (a monarch's deputy), apparently thought the deal was legitimate. A senior Sheraton vice president flew from Boston to Honolulu for a
meeting with the principals, who failed to materialize.
Then Sheraton officials scheduled a meeting in New
York that was postponed after a phone call from Seattle
saying the principals would be a day late.

The meeting was never held. The principal—one
Sammy Amalu—had been arrested in Seattle for writing the worthless $200 check in California.

Sammy, who once duped San Francisco high society into thinking he was a maharaja, has never explained his reasons for the hoax. But Mr. Buchwach, his
editor, figures "he wanted to demonstrate that if you
offer enough money you can tempt anyone. He didn't
swindle anyone. He wanted to prove to himself and the
people of Hawaii that the bigger and richer the corporation, the more gullible it is."

Sheraton was not the only gullible one. Newspapers
reported the deal as if it were fact. On May 10, 1962, The
Wall Street Journal, for instance, reported "Swiss firm
to buy Sheraton's 4 Honolulu Hotels for $34 Million."
The eight-paragraph story quoted a "spokesman" for the
mythical Swiss concern who "confirmed" that an agreement had been made.

Even prison didn't stop Sammy's exploits. In 1966
he got hold of a blank check, filled it out for $175,000
and persuaded a prison employe to cash it for a 10%
cut. The employe was stopped before he could leave the
prison.

Sammy's columns have been "very well received,"
says Mr. Twigg-Smith. "They make great conversation
at cocktail parties." He admits, though, that "some people get annoyed that we let him speak about anything."

James M. Couey Jr., executive editor of the Honolulu Star-Bulletin, the Advertiser's competition, says Sammy's columns offend his "sense of decency."

And at least once they offended Sammy's wardens at Folsom. In 1968 prison authorities shut Sammy's column down on the ground that it violated prison regulations. Mr. Twigg-Smith suspects that pressure was applied by Hawaiian prison officials after Sammy opposed a proposal for a new prison in Hawaii. Mr. Twigg-Smith and other supporters argued the column was an effective part of Sammy's rehabilitation, and after three months he was allowed to resume his writings.

Among his defenders was George T. Davis, a San Francisco lawyer and the victim of Sammy's phony $200 check. Mr. Davis says he swore out the warrant for Sammy's arrest in 1962 "just to teach him a lesson that I think he's learned—don't write your lawyer a bum check."

Right now, Sammy is waiting for a parole board hearing that may make him a free man and give him the chance to make good his threat to run for governor of Hawaii on a "Restore the Monarchy" platform. Sammy feels strongly that the combination of democracy and capitalism has elevated the wrong people to power.

When he is released, Sammy may, if he wishes, step into a full-time writing job with the Advertiser at about $10,000 a year, says Mr. Twigg-Smith. Currently, he's paid on a space-rate basis and makes "very little." Part of his small wage goes to the Folsom Prison recreation fund—"That was part of the deal to get his column back," says Mr. Twigg-Smith—and most of the rest he sends to people he has read about with problems.

—JAMES E. BYLIN

Strange Company

THE Baptist Foundation of America Inc. has always turned a benevolent face to the public—that of a tax-exempt, non-profit organization "born to assist worthy institutions in their struggles to meet the challenge of our times, born to do good for all men."

From its beginning in 1966, it has had an aura of respectability. It has no formal affiliation with any major Baptist group—a spokesman for the Southern Baptist Convention goes to some length to make this point clear—but its co-founder and president, the Rev. T. Sherron Jackson, is a respected Baptist churchman, and its nine-man board of trustees includes five other ministers. Within a short time after its founding, the foundation, which is headquartered in a comfortable suite of offices in Los Angeles, produced a healthy looking balance sheet showing more than $20 million in assets.

It had grand plans. It said it was going to build hospitals for children, retirement centers for the aged and other facilities. It was to be no less than "a monument to faith in God and to freedom and courage of the human spirit."

It hasn't worked out that way. A five-month investigation of the foundation and its nation-wide dealings discloses a different picture—and lends irony to the words of the Old Testament book of Habakkuk, which the foundation quoted in its first brochure: "For I am doing a work in your days that you would not believe if told."

Among other things, the foundation figures in two bizarre stock deals. It has dealt with a string of promoters and men with criminal records. Though it claims disbursement of donations and grants totaling more than $240,000, it has built no children's hospitals, no retirement centers.

The foundation's executives say the financial difficulties and controversies that now trouble BFA are traceable in large measure to men with whom it dealt in good faith—only to be taken for a ride. "I firmly believe that they (the foundation's trustees) were incredibly naive," says Harvey Himmel, BFA's lawyer. "I have a natural inclination to trust people," says Mr. Jackson. "I believed the people we got involved with wanted to help us, but they only used us."

An investigation into the foundation's financial affairs, however, suggests that BFA has been as much a victimizer as it has been a victim. Its financial transactions are now being probed by the California attorney general, the Securities and Exchange Commission, the Internal Revenue Service, the Post Office Department and the Justice Department.

What is known already clearly indicates that the foundation took certain actions that ultimately led to considerable financial losses for individuals and institutions throughout the U.S. Chief among these actions was the issue of countless millions of dollars worth of promissory notes in exchange for property and services. Many of these notes and other obligations are now in default.

The foundation issued these notes on the general

strength of its assets, the value of which was questionable in many cases. Indeed, some of these assets seem not to exist at all. Just how many notes the foundation issued, and for what amount, cannot be determined exactly, although notes totaling in excess of $10 million have surfaced at one time or another. Asked for a complete list of notes, George Magee, controller, says: "It's not normal business procedure to turn over your books and records to newspapers."

In one deal, the foundation agreed to buy an inn in California for, among other things, notes backed by assets that were supposed to include thousands of acres of land in Tennessee. But that agreement was canceled when the foundation couldn't prove to the satisfaction of the seller that the land was owned by BFA. "Our people went there to check, and the assessor just laughed when they asked about it," says a spokesman for the would-be seller of the inn.

It is impossible to find any of the foundation's purported land holdings in Tennessee. The biggest block claimed is 52,739 acres in Cumberland County. BFA, which says a bank in the area has valued the property at a minimum of $45 an acre, has carried it at $20 an acre, for a total value of $1,054,000. But Garland Brown, Cumberland County tax assessor, can't even find it.

"Very poorly described," says Mr. Brown. "We wouldn't even know in which direction to go from the county courthouse to locate it." Besides, he says, the county has finished an extensive property remapping and all its land is accounted for. BFA has never appeared as an owner and has never been on the tax rolls. "It's an impossibility for that land to be here," declares Mr. Brown—who adds that he would certainly know if it were, since the tract would cover one-seventh of the whole county. It's unclear just how BFA came to list this land as an asset.

BFA also doesn't appear as a property taxpayer in Marion County, where it purports to own 6,000 acres, and Warren County, where it claims another 5,000. The Marion County land is supposedly a gift from two men with whom the foundation has had other contact—David Pedley, who deeded 1,000 acres to BFA in November 1967 in his capacity as president of Wilco Land Co., and Nat Rosenberg, who deeded 5,000 acres to BFA in February 1968.

Both men are among those who the foundation's executives say have taken advantage of the foundation, and the men appear as defendants in legal actions BFA has filed in Los Angeles city courts. Neither man has been available to talk to reporters about his involvement with the foundation. Foundation executives assert that many of the transactions BFA became involved in were the result of actions by Rosenberg, a nimble promoter who has been arrested several times and convicted once for passing bad checks.

If the foundation was continually getting taken in by Rosenberg, why did it keep dealing with him? "To tell you the truth," says the Rev. Mr. Jackson, "Rosenberg kept promising to convert to Christianity, so I stayed with him for a time hoping he would do it." He says the foundation severed all ties with Rosenberg in 1968.

It's unclear just what has prompted the foundation to become entangled in so many questionable deals and unusual schemes, and it's unclear what prompted it to produce such a questionable balance sheet. A minister who knows the leaders of the foundation has this theory: "Everyone at BFA wanted to build a big, rich foundation fast and shut their eyes to some of the things that were going on." Mr. Jackson, the foundation president, says: "The Baptists don't have a charitable foundation like other denominations, and we thought we could do it. We are going to continue trying."

Those persons involved in the foundation who are willing to talk to reporters say they have not profited personally from the association. And, indeed, foundation officials do not appear to live extravagantly. Federal investigators, however, are trying to determine if anyone has profited personally from the dealings.

One man who says he has lost a lot of money as a result of the foundation is Walter Dilbeck of Evansville, Ind. A World War II hero who did well in business on his return to civilian life, Mr. Dilbeck decided to set up the Global Baseball League, a league with U.S. and foreign teams. Mr. Dilbeck asserts that he and his friends put $3 million into the league, which began operating in 1967 on a limited scale.

That wasn't enough money, and the league began to founder. Mr. Dilbeck felt that it was a good idea, though, and that the league would prosper if it had a richer owner. Somehow, the foundation became interested. "Anything that promotes good clean minds and bodies is all to the good for the country," Mr. Jackson was quoted as saying in an Associated Press dispatch at the time. He especially liked league rules that required players to work out vigorously and to be in bed by 10:30 p.m. And so early in 1969 the foundation agreed to buy the league for $3 million in foundation notes. At the time, the fledgling league had teams in Japan, Mexico, Puerto Rico, Alabama, New Jersey and Venezuela.

Mr. Dilbeck says the deal was completed in East St. Louis, Ill., on Jan. 12, 1969, with Mr. Jackson and the Rev. S. T. Sullivan, a vice president of the foundation, representing BFA. "They gave me a statement that showed $23 million in assets," Mr. Dilbeck asserts. "And they showed me a brochure, which was the thing that sold me more than anything. There were names in the brochure that I just believed wouldn't be parties to anything that wasn't right."

The name that impressed him most, he says, was that of William Newberg, former president of Chrysler Corp. who was listed as a member of BFA's advisory board. Mr. Newberg, who left Chrysler in 1960 after it was disclosed he had a financial interest in some of Chrysler's suppliers, says he served briefly as a financial adviser to the foundation but ended his connection with it long before the foundation's dealings with Mr. Dilbeck began.

Mr. Jackson says neither he nor anyone else at the foundation ever showed a balance sheet to Mr. Dilbeck. The foundation official says Mr. Dilbeck had his own investigation of the foundation's finances made by a private concern.

At any rate, Mr. Dilbeck sold his league and a lake in Kentucky to the foundation and received $3,860,000 in notes. The only problem, says Mr. Dilbeck, is that he couldn't turn the notes into cash. He tried to discount them, but, he says, nobody would take them. "I sent them to the different insurance companies, and they wouldn't honor them. The local banks wouldn't honor them after they dug into the background of the foundation."

Early in 1970 Mr. Dilbeck sold $3 million of notes (representing the price of the league) back to the foundation for 147,000 shares of Standard Computer & Pictures Corp. stock, which the foundation was holding. Standard's parent company, a private holding firm in North Miami Beach, has guaranteed to buy back the stock at $10 a share if Mr. Dilbeck wants to sell, he says. The stock is currently unregistered, and on Dec. 24, 1969, the Securities and Exchange Commission filed a complaint charging that the parent company, the subsidiary and the man who controlled them had violated registration and antifraud provisions of the securities laws. The defendants were enjoined against such acts by a Federal judge in Miami on Dec. 30. They consented to the injunction but admitted no wrongdoing.

So Mr. Dilbeck now has $860,000 in BFA notes and 147,000 shares of unregistered stock, and the foundation has a lake and a baseball league that owns some teams but has no games scheduled. The foundation also has on its books an asset it values at $4.1 million, which represents an investment by it of perhaps as little as $150,000. (It paid about $1 a share for much of the Standard Computer & Pictures Corp. stock.)

Foundation officials say they offered to buy back their $3 million in notes for stock with a present maximum value of $1,470,000 because they decided the league wasn't worth $3 million. Mr. Dilbeck and his friends took the lesser amount because "we figured that $1.5 million in letter stock is much better than $3 million in BFA notes seeing as we couldn't get a dime on them."

Another asset that has been listed on the foundation's books is a California mining property listed at $7.5 million. Mr. Magee, the foundation controller, says an appraisal by a Las Vegas concern values the property at $12 million, conservatively, an appraisal based on a geologist's report. The geologist's report is incomplete, however. The county tax assessor's office lists the property at a fair market value of $1,600. The mine's last production was in 1966 and amounted to 13 tons of antimony ore worth about $17,000, county records show.

The foundation insists the mine is still a valuable property, however.

Most of the foundation's dealings are incredibly complex, and nearly all involve the issuance of notes by the foundation. The notes, backed by the questionable assets, can prove difficult to convert into cash through traditional channels, as Mr. Dilbeck of the baseball league discovered. Many BFA notes have later turned up in controversial transactions throughout the country. Some BFA notes are still in circulation. Attempts to use BFA notes as collateral for hefty bank loans have been made in New York, Rhode Island, New Jersey and Florida.

Some $600,000 in BFA notes showed up in 1969 in the inflated assets of the Community National Life Insurance Co. of Tulsa, Okla., for example. In the fall of 1969 several executives of that company were indicted by a Federal grand jury in New York for allegedly conspiring to bilk banks and other lending institutions through the fraudulent use of life insurance policies as collateral for loans. All defendants either pleaded guilty or were convicted.

The foundation was not directly involved in this action, but it has been named as a defendant in some others. In 1969 it and its potential convert, Nat Rosenberg, were among 24 individuals and groups enjoined by a Federal court in Baltimore from further violations of the securities laws. Rosenberg and the BFA consented to the injunction but didn't admit any wrongdoing. What the defendants did, according to the SEC, was to pledge unregistered stock whose value had been falsely inflated for "at least $700,000" in loans from banks throughout the U.S. All the loans are in default. Neither the foundation nor Rosenberg were accused of inflating the stock's value.

The stock involved in the case was American Continental Industries Inc., which has since gone into bankruptcy proceedings. The foundation says it got its stock from Rosenberg, though it isn't clear whether the stock came as a gift for notes or for cash. The foundation apparently got 10,000 American Continental shares, and it pledged these as collateral for a $90,000 loan at the Progress National Bank in Toledo, Ohio.

This loan to the foundation is in default, as are three other $90,000 loans that officials of the bank contend were guaranteed by the foundation. The proceeds from one of these three disputed additional loans went to Rosenberg. The bank says the foundation is responsible because Rosenberg pledged a $1,116,000 foundation note as collateral for the loan. The bank is suing the foundation in local courts in California to collect all four loans.

Foundation officials deny any responsibility for the three additional loans. A lawyer for the foundation says the BFA is willing to repay $57,000 to settle the first $90,000 loan. The $57,000 was all the foundation received from the bank, this lawyer says. The additional $33,000 was taken as "brokers' fees" by friends of Rosenberg, the Rev. Mr. Jackson maintains.

Another of the many recipients of foundation notes was a company called Datacomp Service Corp. When BFA became involved in Datacomp, the company was controlled by Seymour Pollack, a promoter who is currently serving a one-to-ten year sentence in California for a loan swindle. Datacomp, which was based in Fort Lee, N.J., was formed in 1967, with 60% of the stock going to a group headed by Pollack. (Another member of the group was Salvator Badalamente, reputedly a lieutenant in one of New York's Mafia families.)

Shortly after it was formed, Datacomp issued 100,-

000 shares of unregistered stock to BFA for $750,000 in BFA notes. A few months later, Datacomp's assets were bought by Dumont Corp., a company with real estate and other interests, for almost 70% of Dumont's stock —thus giving control of Dumont to Pollack. (At the time Pollack was dealing with BFA, he had already been convicted of fraud. Mr. Jackson says he was unaware of this then. He says he was introduced to Pollack by Rosenberg.)

The foundation ultimately wound up with 250,000 shares of Dumont stock in exchange for its Datacomp shares. It took 50,000 of these shares and pledged them for a $282,000 loan from Nationwide Investment Corp. in Los Angeles. Nationwide and BFA are engaged in a series of legal battles over the loan, but BFA executives say they intend eventually to make payments on the loan. Dumont is currently in bankruptcy proceedings.

The Securities and Exchange Commission filed a complaint in Federal district court in New York in 1969 charging that between May and October of 1968 approximately 356,000 shares of unregistered Dumont stock were sold or pledged for about $2.4 million by a number of groups and individuals. BFA was one of the groups mentioned. An injunction was issued barring further violations of the securities laws. BFA consented to the injunction but didn't admit any wrongdoing.

Executives of BFA say they currently are trying to untangle their admittedly complex dealings and to accomplish what is their stated aim: Doing good for others. In its efforts to get straightened out, the foundation is receiving help from Samuel Calabrese.

Mr. Calabrese heads a North Miami Beach company called Computerealty Corp., the private holding firm that controls Standard Computer & Pictures Corp.

Standard Computer is the stock that the foundation traded to Mr. Dilbeck of the baseball league.

Mr. Calabrese and the foundation have had extensive dealings. In 1969 the foundation sold a building it owned in Los Angeles to Computerealty for 100,000 shares of stock in Standard Computer. Computerealty guaranteed it would buy back the Standard Computer stock for $8 a share if the foundation ever wanted to get rid of it and couldn't find a higher price elsewhere.

Subsequently, BFA bought another 125,000 shares of Standard Computer stock from Computerealty for about $1 a share, part of which was paid in notes, Mr. Calabrese says. Why did BFA get such a good deal, considering that other shares of Standard Computer were guaranteed at $8 a share? "Under a private placement like this, with restricted stock, there really isn't a ready market," responds Mr. Calabrese. "So I, as a humanitarian gesture, so to speak, gave it at $1 a share."

It isn't known at what price the foundation carries this stock on its books. What is known, however, is that at the moment the foundation might be rich in listed assets but is poor in cash. "One day, we have a couple of thousand in the bank, and another day we have $50,000," Mr. Magee, the controller, said one day recently. "Today, we are down to a couple of thousand."

—WILLIAM BLUNDELL
and NICHOLAS GAGE

The Old Gang

"**N**O more of this stuff like sending girls up to the rooms of VIPs," declares a chief lieutenant of Howard Hughes in Las Vegas. "We've given this town a massive infusion of legitimacy as well as money."

Thus assured, a visitor leaves the Hughes official and goes to his hotel room—where he gets a telephone call a few minutes later from a hotel functionary in the Hughes organization. Would the visitor (hardly a VIP) like a girl sent up?

That's the way it is in Las Vegas these days. On the one hand, Mr. Hughes has made giant strides toward polishing the tawdry image of the desert playground— aided by a flock of other "legitimate" individual and corporate investors that have followed his lead in buying out a number of Mafia-connected combines that previously owned many of the city's hotels and casinos. The new owners are putting unaccustomed emphasis on attracting the family tourist trade. They have toned down some of the gamier nightclub shows and even begun to promote tourist attractions other than the gambling tables and sparkling nightlife. Gov. Paul Laxalt hails their arrival as "the salvation of Nevada gambling."

But as the hotel employe's offer of a prostitute suggests, much of the Las Vegas cleanup so far is illusion. In fact, the day-to-day operations of the city's gambling palaces still remain largely in the control of men with mobster backgrounds—even though the ownership of most of the casinos has changed hands. Moreover, there are clear indications that some of the "clean new corporate money" recently pumped into Las Vegas is neither wholly new nor wholly clean.

Since 1966, when Mr. Hughes arrived from Boston aboard a private rail car, he has bought some $200 million worth of land, hotels and casinos. Federal investigators were greatly heartened—and Las Vegas old-timers were awed—when the Hughes organization acquired the Desert Inn Hotel and Casino in 1967 and promptly ejected a herd of unsavory characters.

But similar cleanups have failed to accompany Mr. Hughes' subsequent purchases of five other casinos. At the Hughes-owned Sands Hotel and Casino, for example, two men with long-time-mobster connections are still very much in evidence.

One is Mario Marino, the catering manager at the Sands—and, according to Federal agents, a former lieutenant of Gulf Coast Mafia chieftain Carlos Marcello, who was convicted in 1968 of assaulting an FBI agent.

Another Sands employe is Charlie Baron, who used to be a part owner of the place and now works as a shift boss—one of several men who take turns supervising all gambling operations during the casino's 24-hour day. Baron was associated with the old Capone gang in Chicago and at one time was included in a list of 42 powerful mobsters compiled by Treasury agents.

Baron was a part owner of the Tropicana Hotel and Casino when it opened in Las Vegas in 1956. A year later, one of the operating partners, Louis Lederer, was bounced out of Nevada gaming after state authorities charged he was "fronting" for a couple of silent partners—Carlos Marcello and Frank Costello, another well-known racketeer.

Baron also was a founding partner in the Sands in 1952, though he sold his interest before Mr. Hughes bought the place. The other original owners included Meyer Lansky, a key figure in organized crime in the U.S. and the Caribbean; Jake Freedman, gambling boss of Houston, and Isadore (Kid Cann) Blumenfeld, underworld chief in Minneapolis.

Just down the famous Las Vegas "Strip" from the Sands is Caesars Palace, a highly successful casino built in 1966. Its founders were a group headed by Nathan Jacobson, a Baltimore insurance executive widely respected as one of the "new breed" of honest, orthodox businessmen who are brightening the Las Vegas image.

But the manager of the Caesars Palace casino is Jerome Zarowitz, whose background includes a conviction in the 1950s on a Federal charge of fixing football games for gambling purposes. In the fall of 1965, he and his assistant, Elliot Paul Price, attended a meeting in Palm Springs, Calif., with Ruby Lazarus, who now faces bookmaking charges in New York, and Anthony (Fat Tony) Salerno, a known mobster. Federal agents charged that the meeting concerned Syndicate betting on the World Series, but a grand jury probe of the gathering collapsed after two prostitutes who had been present suddenly refused to testify. Lazarus was indicted and convicted of perjury after it was charged that he had lied to the grand jury, but no other indictments were issued.

Most casino owners admit to the presence of men with mob-connected backgrounds in their establishments. "Many employes have criminal records or associations of one kind or another," says a Hughes official. But many casinos have tightened their security measures to keep tab on these and other employes. At Hughes casinos, for example, computers now record the flow of cash across individual gaming tables and bars, and hidden overhead cameras never stop watching gamblers—and employes.

But why not play it even safer and clean out all the men with shady pasts? Hughes people say that such men are too valuable to lose; no one else knows as much about running gambling operations. The owner of one non-Hughes casino agrees. "We couldn't learn in a lifetime what some of these old-timers know almost instinctively—like when to give a high roller more credit and when to shut him off," he says.

Hy Goldbaum is one of these men. He is credit manager of the Stardust Hotel and Casino, owned by Parvin-Dohrmann Corp. of Los Angeles, a company that has been in the news lately because of alleged irregularities in stock transactions by its chairman. As credit manager of the Stardust, Goldbaum decides whether to issue credit to gamblers who run short of luck and money. His police record lists seven aliases and 14 convictions for bookmaking, assault, Federal income tax evasion and other offenses.

His employer, Parvin-Dohrmann, had until recently been characterized by state officials as a "fine example" of the "new, clean" corporate investors in Las Vegas. Local law enforcement officials don't seem perturbed by the failure of such concerns to purge known underworld figures from their employ.

"What the hell," says one top Las Vegas lawman. "Them guys you're naming off are small potatoes. The important thing is that the guys at the top are clean. Let me tell you, a list of casino landlords today sounds like a 'Who's Who' of big business."

That may be true in most cases. But state investigators recently have been giving closer scrutiny to some corporate investors—Parvin-Dohrmann, for one.

The company isn't entirely new to Las Vegas, to begin with. It was selling equipment to Strip hotels back in the 1950s, though it didn't buy its first hotel-casino, the Fremont, until 1966.

The Fremont was bought from Edward Levinson, a Florida and Kentucky bookmaker who was president of the Fremont, and Edward Torres, who was described in 1964 Senate hearing testimony as a racketeer and business partner of Bobby Baker, former Senate aide convicted in 1967 of several criminal charges arising from misconduct in his job. Torres was vice president of the Fremont. Both Torres and Levinson were under Federal investigation at the time of the sale.

The sales agreement called for both Levinson and Torres to remain on the Parvin-Dorhmann payroll at annual salaries of $100,000, but it barred them from direct connections with gambling operations at the Fremont. In May 1967, both were indicted for skimming—siphoning off part of the gambling gross to evade full taxation—during the time they owned the Fremont. In March 1968, Levinson pleaded no contest and was fined $5,000 in Federal court. Charges against Torres were dropped in return for the dropping of an invasion of privacy suit by Levinson against the FBI. Levinson had charged that agents obtained evidence against him illegally through electronic eavesdropping.

Levinson left Parvin-Dohrmann's employ shortly afterward, but Torres continued to manage hotel operations at the Fremont and at the Aladdin, another hotel-casino that was bought by Parvin-Dohrmann in 1968. He became a substantial shareholder in the company. Among his holdings: 10,000 common shares sold to him in July 1968 from the company treasury for

$189,000—at a time when they had a market value of more than $250,000.

The Nevada Gaming Control Board launched an investigation of Parvin-Dohrmann after the Securities and Exchange Commission and the American Stock Exchange both instituted action against the company over stock transactions by its chairman, Delbert Coleman. Trading of Parvin-Dohrmann stock was suspended both on the American exchange and in the over-the-counter market for a time. Though trading was permitted to resume, both the SEC and the exchange stressed that they were continuing their investigations.

Under prodding by the SEC, Mr. Coleman admitted he had sold some 12½% of the company's stock, which he personally held, without notifying either the SEC or the Nevada Gaming Control Board as required under their regulations.

The Gaming Control Board announced it has forbidden Parvin-Dohrmann to acquire any more casinos for an indefinite period, thereby postponing—and perhaps preventing altogether—the company's planned acquisition of the Riviera Hotel and Casino from a group of former Parvin-Dohrmann officers and directors.

Another company whose activities have attracted the interest of state investigators is Continental Connector Corp., a New York-based concern that bought the Dunes Hotel and Casino and has announced plans to acquire the Golden Nugget Casino. A close look at Continental Connector's purchase of the Dunes raises the question of just who took over whom. Certain of the former owner-operators of the Dunes became sizable stockholders and executives of Continental Connector —while their operating control over the hotel-casino remained as firm as ever.

Continental Connector acquired the Dunes in 1969 for $60 million worth of convertible preferred stock. Three men who had held 68% of the hotel-casino became the principal beneficiaries of the deal. They were Major Riddle, president and 35% owner; Sidney Wyman, vice president and 21% owner, and Charles (Kewpie) Rich, vice president and 12% owner.

Mr. Riddle, an oil man and part owner of several night clubs, became a director and 15% owner of Continental Connector. Rich remained a vice president of the Dunes and was elected to the board of Continental Connector; he ended up with 5% of the company's outstanding common stock.

Wyman became president, chairman and chief executive officer of the Dunes. What's more, under terms of the acquisition he was given "complete and sole" control over management of the Dunes for five years, with power to designate seven of the nine board members of the Continental Connector subsidiary (M&R Investment Co.) that runs the hotel-casino. He gained a 9% interest in Continental Connector in the acquisition.

Wyman and Rich have been identified in Senate testimony as former St. Louis bookmakers who bribed Western Union employes in order to use the company's telegraph facilities to place bets. They were part of a group that bought the Riviera Hotel and Casino in 1955 and hired Gus Greenbaum, former manager of the Flamingo Hotel and Casino, to manage the Riviera. For three years, the Riviera's profits failed to meet expectations. In December 1958, Greenbaum and his wife were found dead in their home, their throats slit and a bloody butcher knife nearby. Their killer or killers were never caught.

Another investor who joined Wyman and Rich in the Riviera was Israel (Ice Pick Willie) Alderman, who has a record of arrests dating back to the 1920s on charges of murder, assault, robbery and larceny—but whose only conviction (on an extortion charge) was recently remanded by the Supreme Court to a lower court for retrial.

Wyman and Rich sold out their interest in the Riviera in late 1960, and in 1961 they bought into the Dunes. Mr. Riddle had bought his interest in the Dunes five years earlier.

The sale of the Dunes to Continental Connector turned out to be a useful deal for several other men besides Wyman, Rich and Mr. Riddle. Proxy materials issued in connection with the acquisition make it clear that some of the investors who controlled Continental Connector saw the transaction as considerably more than just a means of possible future profit for the parent company.

Though Continental Connector is relatively new to Las Vegas, control of the company was acquired early in 1968 by a group of men who scarcely rank as newcomers. The men, who paid $4.8 million for their controlling interest, are 24 long-time Las Vegas investors headed by E. Parry Thomas, president of the Bank of Las Vegas.

The Bank of Las Vegas has been a prime source of loans to casinos—including the Dunes—for many years. In fact, when the Dunes was acquired it owed the bank $14.1 million. It also owed another $1.8 million to American National Insurance Co., headed by R. A. Furbush and William Vogler, both members of the Thomas group that had acquired control of Continental Connector.

As part of the purchase agreement, the debts of the Dunes to both the bank and the insurance company were to be paid off in full—by Continental Connector.

The net effect of the whole tangled affair: The Thomas group spent $4.8 million to get effective control of a publicly held company, which was then used to acquire the Dunes and repay the Dunes' debts of $15.9 million to organizations run by members of the Thomas group. In the process, some old owner-managers of the Dunes were greatly enriched while remaining deeply entrenched in its operation—and while being elevated to positions of importance within the new parent company.

Despite the continued presence of mobsters and the tangled affairs of some of the corporate investors, Nevada officials and legislators have been so impressed with the flood of new investors that they recently changed their laws to facilitate it. Previously, the state required investigation and licensing of all would-be casino owners. But this is obviously a monumental task when a publicly held company with millions of shareholders is involved, so the requirements have been eased to cover only individuals who own 5% or more of a casino.

Gov. Laxalt, who fought hard for the changes, says they will "minimize the so-called underworld taint" by encouraging corporate investors. Others aren't so sure. George Dickerson, a Las Vegas lawyer who quit as chairman of the Nevada Gaming Commission when the rules were changed, fears that the new law only takes from the state what power it had to determine who really owns and runs the casinos.

Though Las Vegas is still far from "clean," the public seems to be reacting favorably to what one cab driver calls "the Hughes effect." Total casino revenues in 1968 rose 35% from 1967, and several new hotels and casinos are being built. Hotel occupancy was running around 90% in 1968, compared with an average of 70% from 1960 to 1967.

To be sure, many of the familiar fixtures are still around—middle-aged sugar daddies with show girls in tow, battalions of old ladies force-feeding the slot machines, prostitutes who sometimes carry walkie-talkies to coordinate their appointments.

But the efforts to attract a growing family trade appear to be working. One effect: Las Vegas now draws tourists from parts of the country that rarely contributed visitors in the past. With amazement, an official of the Sands says, "We ran a check and found 28% of our customers are from the *Midwest.*" For years, about 80% of Las Vegas' visitors came from the Los Angeles area, and the rest came mainly from New York and Texas.

Catering to the newcomers, several Strip establishments are de-emphasizing the usual gaudy, bare-bosomed stage shows and instead offering "family entertainment," including adaptations of Broadway musicals. Veteran comic Jack Carter says he has had to drop several gags from his routine because they are too blue or too "subtle" for the new audiences.

The rough stuff that often occurred in the old Las Vegas also seems to be disappearing. Recently a blackjack dealer in a Hughes casino was caught cheating the house. Strip veterans claim they were amazed when the managers called the police and had the dealer arrested. In the old days, the veterans contend, the fellow probably would have had his hands smashed with a baseball bat.

Even some of the Federal agents who have been watching and pursuing Las Vegas hoodlums for decades admit the city is changing for the better, despite the many continuing problems. "Spend 20 years tracking down these crumbs and you begin to distrust your own grandmother," says one agent. "But Las Vegas isn't the same old town. I can't deny it. It's gradually moving toward a more honest, businesslike economy." Then he pauses and adds a qualification: "Very gradually."

—STEVEN M. LOVELADY

"This Is a Stick-up"

MAYBE it's all due to Bonnie and Clyde.

Nobody seems to have any more convincing explanation for a fantastic rise in bank robberies across the country. Some blame it on bank architecture that makes robberies easier, some blame it on the spread of branch banking to rural areas where get-aways are quicker, and some simply cite the population boom, figuring the more people there are the more bank robbers there are.

One enforcement official sneers and says: "It's the easy-living generation. Everyone's living high off the hog. By the time a bum's 35, if he hasn't earned it, he'll try to steal it."

Whatever the reason, the situation is almost getting out of hand. The Federal Bureau of Investigation says there were 1,730 robberies of banks and other savings institutions in 1967—about 7 each banking day— up 50% from 1,164 in 1966 and a six-fold jump from the 278 of 1957. The year-to-year increase was by far the biggest jump in any category of crime.

One bank, an Oxon Hill, Md., branch of the Southern Maryland Bank & Trust Co., was hit six times in less than 2½ years. The modern brick structure recently closed permanently because employes refused to work there any longer. It was the first time since the

1940s that a bank has closed because of robberies, according to the American Bankers Association.

It's not that banks are trying to make things easier for the crooks. In fact, there are all kinds of new methods to discourage attempts at bank robbing, ranging from "loaded" bills that discharge tear gas as the robber escapes to window decals that warn "Except ye repent, ye shall all perish."

But the robbers aren't deterred. The closed Oxon Hill bank had a silent alarm system and surveillance cameras, among other sophisticated devices, yet the perpetrators of only one of the six heists have been caught. "The robbers apparently were coming from Washington. They would knock us off and go back and get lost," says George M. Sullivan, senior vice president of Southern Maryland Bank & Trust.

The six hauls cost the bank less than $50,000—"We were very fortunate," says Mr. Sullivan—but they caused the bank a lot of grief. "Our employes were abused and pistol whipped. They refused to work any longer," he says. A woman customer, making her first visit to the bank, was thrown to the floor, robbed and held at gunpoint. Frightened customers began withdrawing their deposits. Eventually, the bond that covered losses was canceled by the insurance company.

The FBI doesn't announce figures for losses from bank robberies, but the American Bankers Association says banks lost $3,323,000 to robbers in the first half of 1967, up from $1,900,000 a year earlier.

Insurance companies, not the banks, generally are stuck with the robbery losses, and they're not happy about the increase. "Banks aren't generally regarded as creampuff risks anymore," says one insurance man. A spokesman for Insurance Co. of North America says the "bank insurance business has been generally unprofitable over the past few years." And an officer of Aetna Casualty & Surety Co. says, "We've become a little numb, we've been hit so badly."

As a result, insurers are pressing for industry-wide increases in premiums on bankers' blanket bonds, which cover robbery, burglary and embezzlement losses. An increase would be the first since 1961. For years prior to that, the rates had been declining. The extent of any increase hasn't been worked out yet, but one insurance official says that "bankers might be considerably surprised."

Bankers say they're doing all they can to stop the hold-ups. Many banks are forming special security departments, often headed by former FBI agents. The FBI itself has stepped up its program of briefing bankers on how to prevent—and handle—bank robberies. And the Justice Department, concerned by the trend, is drafting legislation that would require banks to have at least some robbery-prevention equipment.

Most larger banks conduct special training sessions for tellers and managers, telling them what to do when they're slipped a note that says "This is a stick-up." Generally, tellers are told to cooperate and to keep quiet: a White Plains, N.Y., teller was shot when she told a robber, "You must be kidding."

William Barry, chief of security for Bankers Trust Co. in New York, stresses the importance of getting an accurate description of the hold-up men. During training sessions, Mr. Barry has someone stage a mock hold-up. Afterwards, he asks for descriptions. "Usually they're hilarious," he says. One example: "He had a married man's stomach."

It wouldn't be hard to identify a hold-up man if he happened to steal a packet of bills supplied by Property Protection Service of America. The bills contain two vials that, when broken, release a strong scent that clings to the bandit.

The Decatur, Ga., firm also keeps three dogs that are trained to follow the scent, but so far they haven't been needed because there has been only one hold-up at a bank using the packets. That bank didn't ask for the dogs. (Nor did that bank have the warning decal—with the Biblical quotation—that the Georgia company provides its clients.)

Bills timed to release tear gas have proven effective, according to Walter A. Williamson, president of U.S. Currency Protection Corp. of Scottsdale, Ariz. He says one bandit, who unknowingly placed a "loaded" roll in his shirt, was found later in a basement, cowering behind a boiler. The exploding money had torn a hole in his shirt and sent him into shock.

—EDWARD P. FOLDESSY

Shades of Dillinger

IT was a classic bank holdup. Two armed robbers emptied the bank's tills and raced to their getaway car, which they had left in the bank's parking lot. But the car was stuck on the ice.

One bandit jumped out to push. He got the car moving, but the driver, understandably in a hurry, dragged the pusher 25 feet along the ground before stopping to pick him up. When the battered pusher did get in the car he sat on a shotgun, which went off, critically wounding him. Apparently thinking his partner was trying to do him in and keep the loot for himself, he pulled a gun and shot the driver. When police arrived, both bandits were dead in the car.

Some people in Montreal say the most unusual element of that 1966 heist was that it was solved. For Montreal has nearly as many unsolved bank robberies as it has bank robberies—and that's a lot. In 1968 Montreal had 93 bank robberies, only about a quarter of which had been solved by mid-1969—meaning arrests had been made and the accused had either been convicted or were awaiting trial. In the first four months of 1969, Montreal had 51 bank robberies—only 12 of which were solved.

Perhaps because of the low rate of apprehensions, so many bank robbers have flocked to the charming city that it has become No. 1 in bank robberies in North

America. The 51 in early 1969 compare with 36 in Los Angeles, which the FBI says is the leading U.S. city for bank robberies. Los Angeles police say they solve 60% or more of their bank robberies in the year they occur.

Students of bank heists say Montreal's low rate of arrests isn't due to police ineptitude—though a Montreal policeman did shoot himself in the leg in the confusion that followed the robbery in which the two bandits were found dead. Experts say the police in Montreal have a poor record because Montreal's robbers are more organized and more professional than those elsewhere. They also say that robbers are attracted to Montreal because even if they are caught their sentences are likely to be lighter than they would be in other cities.

"Each city has its own mode of crime," says Dr. Michael Sendbuehler, a Montreal psychiatrist familiar with criminal behavior. He says that while cities like New York and Chicago have organized gangs in the dope, prostitution and protection rackets, most organized gangsters in Montreal apparently prefer to rob banks for a living. Jean-Paul Gilbert, director of the Montreal police, agrees. Observing that the city is relatively free of other types of organized crime, he says, "The gangs in Montreal go in for robbing banks."

Police officials elsewhere in Canada and in major U.S. cities say their bank robberies usually are the work of lone gunmen who pass notes to tellers demanding money. Police say most of these people are desperate, mixed-up individuals who are relatively easy to catch.

"The lone gunman is the guy more likely to be going down hill, who's a washout and very often fantastically stupid," says Dr. Sendbuehler.

Not so with the average Montreal bank robber. Robbers work in teams of three to five members, heavily armed with pistols, sawed-off shotguns and machine guns. Their planning is careful and their timing precise. Knowing that it takes police about three minutes to respond to an alarm, the robbers usually take no more than a minute to leap over the counters and clean out the cash drawers.

Director Gilbert of the police department tells of several gangs who station a man with a watch at the door. Starting at 60, he loudly counts down the seconds "as if he were launching an Apollo," says Mr. Gilbert. When the timer calls out zero, the gang breaks off and runs for the getaway car, which invariably was stolen a short time earlier and which will be abandoned a few blocks from the scene.

These gangs not only are faster than the lone gunman, but also they get more loot. In 1968, the average take in Montreal was $5,000, while the average take in other major cities was $2,000 to $3,000. Of course, robbers in Montreal have to share their proceeds among the whole gang.

If a gang is apprehended and convicted, its members often are back on the street within a few years. Many persons with a record of armed robbery receive only four to seven years in prison, compared with an average sentence of 10 years in Toronto and sentences of 10 to 15 years in many U.S. cities.

"This is a major factor" behind Montreal's high rate of robberies, Director Gilbert claims. "It's a fact that when you have a serious problem, as we have in Montreal, the courts should take this into consideration and hand out heavier sentences."

A detective also questions the practice of letting alleged bank robbers out on bail to await trial. "A lot of these guys go out and rob another bank to pay their lawyers," he claims.

Joe Bedard, former head of the police's holdup squad and now in charge of security for the Royal Bank of Canada and the Bank of Montreal, is also irked by the light sentences. He shows off a watch presented to him by the Canadian Bankers Association in 1960 for having captured the notorious "Red Hood Gang," whose four members were known to have committed some 25 robberies in a four-year period. "And you know something?" he says. "They're all out of jail now."

The banks have added new protective measures—including new alarm systems and heavy glass around tellers' cages—but most bank branches still don't have armed guards. The police claim the bankers, whose losses are covered by insurance, don't want to spend the extra money for more protection. Bankers don't like to discuss the matter, though one does concede that insurance rates have risen sharply in the past two years.

Some banks have been cutting down the money they keep on hand, and the Provincial Bank of Canada has put some tellers in seven branches in locked, bullet-proof cages. "The girl in the cage could sit there and make faces at the robbers if she wanted to, and there'd be no way to get at her," says a bank official. These branches, each of which had been robbed five or six times in the past few years, haven't been held up in the short time the cages have been in use.

But one gang, apparently enamored with the trend toward drive-in banking, might have discovered a way to get to the cages. At least they've found a new way to get into banks.

The three-man gang robbed a Montreal bank of $35,000 by backing a panel truck through the bank's plate glass window shortly after closing. Before the startled employes could react, the truck's rear doors swung open and the trio, armed with semi-automatic rifles, hopped out. After scooping up the cash in the tills, they climbed back through the truck and jumped in their getaway car, which was parked nearby. They made a clean escape.

That gang was imaginative, but it probably won't catch the public fancy as much as another gang that operated until Sept. 19, 1967. It was headed by an attractive mother of three, Machine Gun Molly. Molly, who lived most of her life in the city's red-light district, started her bank-robbing career in 1965 at the age of 27. She began as a driver of getaway cars, but soon was planning and organizing heists for a gang that included two or three men. Police say that in 1967 she took part in at least 20 armed robberies that netted close to $100,-000.

Molly, whose real name was Monique Proietti, used a semiautomatic M-1 carbine embellished with gold leaf. It was capable of firing short bursts with one pull of the trigger, hence her nickname.

Her end came when she was fleeing a bank robbery in which she got $3,000. The getaway car, which was being chased by police through city streets at up to 110 miles an hour, slammed into the side of a bus. A gunfight ensued, and Molly was shot dead.

At the time, a French newspaper in Montreal observed:

"If Al Capone had had a daughter, he would have wanted her to be like Monique Proietti."

—D'ARCY O'CONNOR

The Paper Hangers

CHEMICAL Bank New York Trust Co. detectives have been frustrated so far in pursuing Richard A., who cashed five forged checks worth almost $10,000 there in 1967. They have a description and several addresses for him, and think they may even have seen him face-to-face—but they can't be sure because Richard, a slender clerk, often dresses up as Mary A., a bosomy blond.

"We missed him on Fire Island and several other places," laments Robert Dodge, chief bank security officer. "What can we do when we think we've located our suspect but a woman answers the door?" He vows, however, to track down Richard-Mary again and keep him-her under surveillance until local police can make an arrest. "We'll find him," declares Mr. Dodge. "There aren't many places in the U.S. where this type of person hangs out."

Richard's transvestitism may be the most titillating part of this story, but Mr. Dodge's determination is the newsier part for bankers—and for forgers. Until recently most banks, when stuck with a forged check, would simply pocket the loss or pass it on to their insurance companies. Often, the incidents wouldn't even be reported to police.

But banks can't afford that attitude any more. Though there are no precise figures on how big a haul forgers are making, some sources place the loss to the whole economy at $400 million to $1 billion a year. The American Bankers Association more conservatively estimates the 1968 loss at $70 million—but figures that was up 16% from 1967. And some New York banks think the ABA's percentage figure is low; one says its forgery losses rose 40% in 1968 and another reports a 25% increase.

Banks and insurers can only theorize about the reasons for such increases. Some contend merchants are too willing to accept—and pass along to banks—almost any checks from customers. Others assail courts and prosecutors for alleged leniency in dealing with forgers who get caught, or simply bewail the ethical atmosphere of the times ("the moral fiber of America isn't bent; it's broken," says one insurance man). But at least some banks suspect an additional reason may be that word has been spreading that banks have been pigeons for "paper hangers," criminal jargon for forgers.

The banks say they have nowhere to turn for help, either. Police departments have their hands too full coping with violent crime to spare much time to chase forgers, says an ex-police detective who now works for a bank. And insurers increasingly are writing deductible clauses, limiting their liability to losses above a specified amount, into the policies that protect banks against robbery, embezzlement and other fraud losses.

Deductibles of $5,000 to $25,000 are common, bankers say—and they apply to the loss on any single forged check, not to total forgery losses. Since forgers rarely try to pass single checks for such large amounts—let alone the $1 million that the deductible clause in one Eastern bank's bond is said to specify—the practice means banks increasingly must swallow forgery losses themselves.

So, many banks have been creating or expanding security departments, largely to catch forgers. Chase Manhattan Bank in New York, for example, has doubled its security staff and tripled the staff's budget in the last five years.

The expanded staffs often try to develop a complete case against a suspected forger, track him down and sometimes even apprehend and hold him for local police. "We're actually doing the police investigation" in many cases, says a Bankers Trust Co. security official in New York.

Banks vow, too, to stop the once-common practice of dropping charges against a caught forger who will agree to repay the loss quietly. From now on, many say, they will insist on prosecution.

The job of detecting—and preventing—forgeries is a big one, however. Forgers have developed techniques, ranging from the deceptively simple to the highly sophisticated, in enough variety to win the grudging respect of bank security men.

Richard A.'s technique for defrauding Chemical Bank was simplicity itself. He opened what appeared to be a legitimate account, deposited into it checks that were intended for his employer rather than for him, and wrote his own checks against these deposits. He altered the checks he deposited by typing his own name above the name of his employer as the payee. He escaped detection for over two months because the name of his employer, a major educational corporation, sounded like the name of a residence hall.

More frequently a forger will steal blank checks from individuals or corporations, fill in an amount and a fictitious name as payee, and forge the payer's signature. He then will present the check to a bank at which he has opened an account in the fictitious name. Usually a forger will use the "split-deposit" technique; that is, if he wants to collect, say, $100, he will write himself a forged check for $250 and ask to deposit $150 in the account and collect the remaining $100 in cash. Bank tellers, who might well send a customer seeking to take the entire $250 in cash to a bank officer to present identification, are more likely to accept checks for "split deposit" and hand over the cash without comment.

Forgers who steal checks from individuals usually familiarize themselves with the dates on which major banks mail out monthly statements and canceled checks to checking-account customers. They then loot mailboxes on those dates.

A successful mailbox haul sets the forger up with samples of the account-holder's signature, from canceled checks, and information from the monthly statement on how much money is in the customer's account and how many checks he is likely to write in a month. The forger then obtains blank checks by a variety of methods; one may be to gain admittance to the home by pretending he is a salesman or other caller and steal checks out of a checkbook that the home owner may have left lying on a desk or table.

In stealing blank checks from companies, forgers follow one general rule: Take only a few checks at a time, and always take them from the back of the checkbook, so that the theft will be more likely to go unnoticed for some time. Otherwise, their techniques differ.

One forger that a bank's security department caught regularly visited small firms in New York's garment district pretending he was looking for a job. Sooner or later, he would get in to see a busy executive who would be called away from his office during the interview. The forger would then make a quick search for the company checkbook and slip out a few checks before the executive returned.

Other forgers burglarize corporate offices at night. The more sophisticated take pains to mess up the offices in such a way as to mislead police—they hope—into thinking they were searching for cash and other valuables rather than for checks.

Though many forgers present bad checks directly to banks, others try to palm them off on merchants. Generally the forger will place a big order for merchandise, tell the merchant he needs it immediately but doesn't have much cash on him, and ask if he can pay by check. His hope is that the merchant will be too anxious to ring up the sale to demand proof of identity. If the merchant seems especially cooperative, the forger may ask if he can write a check for somewhat more than the value of the order and take the difference in cash; many a merchant eager for a rich sale will comply.

Banks frequently are eventually stuck with the loss on these checks, too. Generally, the bank on which the check is drawn will receive it from the merchant's bank through normal clearing channels and will pay it by debiting the account of the customer whose name was forged to the check. The fraud then may not be detected until the legitimate customer receives, with his monthly statement, a canceled check he knows he didn't write—and that can be as much as a month later. By then, it's usually too late for the bank to take the matter up with the merchant. Banking laws generally specify that if a bank doesn't detect the forgery in a few days and return the check unpaid to the merchant, it must take the loss.

All the techniques discussed so far, it should be

noted, are those of the free-lance forger. He is the dominant, but not the only, type. Banks say some forgers are members of organized rings that supply them with phony or stolen identification. Some rings even run printing plants that turn out counterfeit checks—complete, in some cases, with magnetically-encoded account numbers that will zip right through a bank's computer.

Banks suspect that some rings are linked to the Mafia. Some use Mafia-style methods. One New York bank tells of catching a forger it suspected of belonging to a ring and coaxing him for weeks to reveal the identity of other members of the syndicate and the location of its check-printing plant. Eventually, the bank says, the forger promised to tell the full story on a Friday. On Thursday his body was found in an upstate field, riddled with bullets.

Banks are putting to work the information their security departments have turned up on forgers' techniques to devise preventive measures. New York's First National City Bank, for instance, recently sponsored a fraud-prevention clinic for 200 Bronx merchants, who heard talks by half a dozen law enforcement experts.

To make things harder for mailbox looters, many banks vary the dates on which they mail monthly checking-account statements. Some also include in the mailings printed warnings not to leave checkbooks lying around where "casual" visitors can pick them up. As a further precaution, some banks advise customers to adopt different signatures for correspondence and for checks—"Robt. Carpenter" for a letter, perhaps, but "Robert S. Carpenter" for checks.

Banks further are beginning to compare notes with each other and with other money handlers on known and suspected forgers. In Detroit, several large banks have signed up with Comp-U-Check Inc., which maintains a computerized pool of information on forgers and other bad-check passers. A bank that obtains a would-be check-casher's driving-license number can telephone while the customer waits and have the number fed into the computer. In seconds it will be told whether the customer's check-cashing record is clear or questionable.

Surveillance cameras installed in bank branches are an effective weapon against the forger who visits the same bank office several times, bankers say. Chemical Bank in New York finally caught one forger, who had passed 150 bad checks totaling $50,000 on a half-dozen New York banks within a year, after he made the mistake of hitting one "camera-bugged" Chemical branch three times.

"By getting tellers' descriptions and comparing them to the films, we were able to identify the suspect," says Mr. Dodge, the security officer. He adds that the suspect confessed after viewing movies of himself taken by the bank's cameras.

Banks have had less success, insurers say, in strengthening their front line of defense against forgery: The tellers to whom many forged checks are presented for cashing or deposit.

Banks have tried to make tellers more watchful. They generally instruct tellers not to cash checks for a customer they do not recognize, but to send the customer to a bank officer to present identification. Many banks also periodically warn branches not to transact any business at all with holders of specific accounts that have been "red-tagged" by the bank as questionable.

The "red-tagging" occasionally is done at the request of law-enforcement authorities. Recently, New York County District Attorney Frank Hogan asked Chase Manhattan to watch for checks drawn on a unit of the Human Resources Administration, New York City's antipoverty agency. Chase eventually received from a Swiss bank, and refused to pay, four checks totaling over $1 million that turned out to have been stolen from an HRA checkbook and forged.

Insurers say, however, that high turnover rates among bank personnel mean few tellers stay on the job long enough to develop careful habits in watching for possible forgery. One New Yorker recently thought he would have some trouble when a new teller at the Wall Street branch of Irving Trust Co. compared his signature on a new check with the signature on a card he had filled out many years before to open his account. His handwriting has changed so much, he says, that the two signatures bore little resemblance to each other. He was surprised when the teller came back to her cage and cashed his check without comment.

—Edward P. Foldessy

The Forger's Best Friend

THE executive who signs his name by quickly scratching a few illegible lines may make himself feel important. He also makes himself a forger's delight, warns Paul A. Osborn, who heads a New York firm that specializes in examining questionable documents.

How should he sign? "The hardest kind of signature to forge is one that contains at least two full names and is written rapidly, freely and legibly," says Mr. Osborn. He adds that the signature should be in normal script, with all the letters connected. A signature with unconnected letters is easier to forge, says Mr. Osborn, because the forger gets a chance to work more slowly, lifting his pen at the breaks while he studies carefully the rest of the letters.

—EDWARD P. FOLDESSY

Hot Stocks

"**F**RED isn't here right now," an official at the big brokerage firm in New York tells a telephone caller. "He's out tapping a phone."

Fred is one of the firm's internal security agents, and security agents are very busy these days. They're trying to cope with a mushrooming problem: Massive, well-organized thefts of stock and bond certificates from brokers' offices.

Fred's side is losing. That's the conclusion that emerges from interviews with brokers, law enforcement officials and stock thieves. They say stealing stocks and bonds is easy. In fact, they say lax security measures, confusion in busy back offices and indifferent book-keeping at many brokerage offices almost invite theft.

There are no precise estimates of how much the thieves are taking. But in 1968 almost 500 of the 650 Big Board member firms reported as "missing" securities valued at about $37 million, up from about $9 million in 1966. Of the $37 million, securities valued at about $12.4 million were listed as definitely stolen, and many of the remaining securities were presumed stolen.

The $12.4 million represents only part of the picture. Observers believe that some firms with embarrassingly high theft losses were among those that didn't file reports. The figure also doesn't reflect losses of smaller brokerage houses not members of the Big Board.

Almost everyone agrees the major reason for the upsurge is the confusion that envelopes most brokerage firms as they struggle with huge paperwork backlogs. The confusion has made stock-stealing so easy that "I don't know why anybody bothers to rob banks anymore," says Andrew J. Maloney, an assistant U.S. Attorney in New York.

Especially vulnerable to theft are certificates owned by investors but held in brokers' offices in the name of the brokerage house. Brokers have long maintained such accounts for regular customers and frequent traders; carrying the securities in these so-called street names saves the broker and the investor a lot of paperwork.

Lately, more and more stock is being handled this way as the brokers seek ways to cut down on their paperwork. One source at E. F. Hutton & Co. estimates that major firms now do 75% of their business in street names, up from 50% five years ago. This concentration of securities in one place makes the crook's job easier. Also, it's easier for thieves to convert street-name stock into cash because banks, which take the certificates as collateral for loans, tend to assume the bearer of such stock is the owner.

Many brokers, whose theft-insurance costs more than doubled between mid-1968 and mid-1969, are clearly concerned. They are tightening their internal security. But observers say they have a long way to go. "The odds very definitely favor the thieves," says Alan I. Baron, an assistant U.S. Attorney in Baltimore.

Who is stealing all the securities? Law enforcement officials say there is mounting evidence that the Mafia is involved. "There can be no doubt about it," says Robert Morgenthau, U.S. Attorney for the southern district of New York. "There is an organized pattern—by organized crime—in the fencing of stolen securities."

Thieves use a variety of tactics to steal stocks. Usually, however, they work in pairs—the outside man plans the theft and sets up the sale of the stolen securities while the inside man actually does the stealing. It apparently is simple to find or plant an inside man.

"I can get a kid off the street, put him in a $125-a-week job in a broker's cage and have my own inside man, just like that," Francis X. Glynn says with a snap of the fingers. Brokerage houses have "lousy prehiring security," says Mr. Glynn, a man who knows of what he speaks. He recently pleaded guilty in a Massachusetts court to possession of stolen stocks. (Mr. Glynn, who aided the state in the prosecution of another defendant in the case, received a suspended sentence.)

Sometimes it's easier to use a person already working at the firm, however. He may be a man in debt to underworld loan sharks, and thus vulnerable to pressure. Or he may be a low-paid clerk or messenger, susceptible to a bribe.

"It's pretty naive to pay a guy $1.75 an hour and expect him to carry around millions of dollars worth of stock all day long and not be tempted to take some," says a security officer for a major brokerage house.

After planting the inside man, the next step is picking the securities to steal—and here the thieves can be very particular. Consider a recent case involving a major brokerage firm:

State investigators and also the firm's security agent say the inside man, a messenger, first stole stocks that were registered in the name of an individual customer. "No, no, we don't want those," the outside man snapped, explaining that he wanted securities listed in the brokerage firm's name. The messenger went back inside. Apparently he couldn't find the right kind of stock certificates, but he did the next best thing, stealing more than $150,000 in bonds listed in the firm's name.

Such thefts aren't as daring as they might appear. In many cases the certificates aren't even locked away. They're stacked all over the broker's office.

"It's unbelievable how cluttered the cage area gets with stock," says a security agent for one broker. "Sometimes, when a file cabinet is moved in order to paint behind it, there is stock lying on the floor." One police official says he has seen stock certificates "on top of filing cabinets, under desks and behind water coolers."

Henryk Nowak, a Montreal detective who recently visted some New York brokers while tracking a stock thief, says he witnessed an appalling lack of office security practices. "It made me sick," he says. "There were far too many people with all-but-unlimited access to the stock certificates."

Sometimes brokers don't even enforce the security provisions they've adopted. A security officer in one big brokerage office in the Northeast says a messenger stole $175,000 in municipal bonds from a strongbox after an office supervisor entrusted the messenger with one of his own duties—seeing to it that the box was locked. The messenger pleaded guilty and awaits sentencing.

In another case, thieves duped the broker's own transfer agent. When 3,000 shares of IBM arrived at the broker's New York office, a clerk didn't record the delivery. Instead, he dispatched the shares to the transfer agent and had the shares registered in the name of, and delivered to, an accomplice. "That was 60 days ago, and both men have long since disappeared," says an investigator for the broker's insurance company.

There are several ways to convert stolen securities into cash. One method, which often involves an intermediary, is to use them as collateral for a bank loan. After getting the loan, the thief and the intermediary try to disappear. That was the plan that Vincent Teresa had.

Teresa, an admitted Boston loan shark, was convicted in April 1968 in Federal District Court in Baltimore of interstate transportation of about $650,000 in bonds stolen from Dean Witter & Co., Manufacturer's Hanover Trust Co. and New York offices of Merrill Lynch, Pierce, Fenner & Smith. Trial records indicate Teresa gave a Baltimore travel agent some $253,000 in bonds, which the agent used as collateral for several loans from a Baltimore bank.

The same case involved another method of converting bonds to cash. Teresa gave $200,000 in bonds to a Baltimore real estate developer, who tried to cash them at Caesars Palace, a Las Vegas casino. But when the casino routinely transmitted the bonds to a Federal Reserve bank, Federal authorities matched them up with a list of stolen bonds, a discovery that led to Teresa's arrest and conviction before he could disappear.

The Baltimore travel agent and real estate developer testified against Teresa and weren't prosecuted. They also voluntarily turned over to prosecutors the approximately $200,000 in bonds they still held. Teresa received a 20-year sentence—one of the stiffest ever handed down in cases of this kind. He is appealing.

Before sentencing Teresa, Baltimore Federal Judge Edward S. Northrop studied a report prepared by Federal investigators, then told Teresa: "The court cannot help but feel that . . . you are connected with the so-called Cosa Nostra and have operated in the same pattern, the same mold and with the same means. . . ."

Nabbing high-ranking Mafia figures in stock theft and fencing cases is very difficult, law enforcement officials say. "From what we see, the really big name hoods keep at least two or three guys between them and the stock transactions at all times," says a New York City detective. "That makes it pretty tough to break down all the links in the chain and get at the final guy in these cases."

Despite this difficulty, Federal investigators have arrested two alleged prominent Mafia figures in New York in cases involving stolen stocks.

On July 29, 1969, the FBI arrested Arthur Tortorello, labeled by prosecutors a loan shark and fence at his arraignment on charges of conspiring to transport $1 million in stolen securities across state lines. A Federal source identifies Tortorello as "one of the more affluent" members of the Carlo Gambino Mafia family in New York. Tortorello is not new to the securities business. He was convicted in 1964 for a conspiracy in the illegal sale and delivery of unregistered stock.

Tortorello's arrest was related to the seizure of some $1 million in stolen securities at New York's Kennedy International Airport on May 29, 1969. Those securities, in turn, are part of a larger batch of $4 million in stocks and bonds pilfered from New York brokerage firms since December 1968, says Mr. Maloney, the assistant U.S. attorney in New York. The other $3 million still hasn't been found.

Prosecutors are expected to allege at the trial that the Tortorello case involves a theft and fencing ring so organized that prospective buyers of stolen stocks could specify which issues they wanted. The ring would then steal the stocks and then even have them transferred into the "customer's" name by the victim broker's legitimate transfer agent, authorities say.

In another case, Anthony Di Lorenzo was charged in New York July 30, 1969, with conspiracy to transport about $1 million in stolen IBM stock from New York to a financially troubled small insurance company in Gettysburg, Pa., in 1967. Jack Kaplan, an assistant U.S. Attorney in New York who is prosecuting the Di Lorenzo case, charged at the arraignment that Di Lorenzo is heir apparent to the leadership of the New York Mafia family identified with the late Vito Genovese. Di Lorenzo is free on a $200,000 bond, pending further prosecution of the case.

Prosecution of stock thieves is difficult because it often takes months for investigators to uncover a theft, giving the thief time to slip away. Even then, brokers often aren't aware that the securities have been missing, investigators complain.

One investigator, for example, tells how he learned through underworld contacts that stocks had been stolen from a San Francisco brokerage office, then phoned the brokers with the news. "They checked, and at first they couldn't even verify the stocks were missing," he says.

Law enforcement officials would like to see stock exchanges require all member firms to report all securities thefts as soon as they are known. "That kind of provision could do nothing but help us," says New York's Mr. Maloney, who says he can't understand why some brokers now don't report all thefts routinely. "I guess it has something to do with embarrassment. I suppose you don't look too good when you announce you've been hit for some six figure amount of stocks, and that was six months ago and you've just found out," he says.

—TIM METZ

Sophisticated Crooks

THIEVES who steal stock on Wall Street are resorting to more sophisticated schemes.

In the past, crooks concentrated mostly on old-fashioned theft, physically removing stock and bond certificates from brokerage offices by stealth or force and then arranging for their sale on the outside.

Now thieves are seeking to master office procedures to dupe firms into freely turning the certificates over to them.

In a case under investigation by Manhattan District Attorney Frank Hogan, two New Yorkers have been charged with using a forged letter and a Swiss bank account in an attempt to swindle $740,000 from Shearson, Hammill & Co., a member of the New York Stock Exchange. Thanks partly to quick action by the brokerage firm in reporting to the law, the alleged scheme failed and the suspects were arrested.

In another case, a corrupt clerk at a brokerage house falsely credited associates with thousands of dollars of stock.

Lawmen estimate that the value of securities stolen from Merrill Lynch, Pierce, Fenner & Smith Inc., Blair & Co. and other brokerage houses and banks have soared to huge amounts in recent years. Attorney General Mitchell told the annual convention of the American Bankers Association that $40 million of stolen stocks and $25 million of stolen or lost Government bonds are currently in circulation.

But, Wall Street has been tightening its security measures to make it tougher for the crooks to break in and steal certificates. "There's more use of guards on the premises, more locks on doors and more employe identification," says Philip Hoblin Jr., first vice president and general counsel for Shearson-Hammill. Mr. Hoblin also notes that brokers are making increasing use of a central, computerized bookkeeping service for recording securities transactions, thereby reducing the actual transfer of certificates from one firm to another.

So the thieves are getting craftier. "False entries into bookkeeping machines, fraudulent accounts and bogus letters are becoming more commonplace on Wall Street," reports William Barry, a veteran investigator, who is president of Smith & Wesson Security Services, retained by Shearson-Hammill to aid in the current investigations. Smith & Wesson is a subsidiary of Bangor Punta Corp.

The alleged scheme to swindle Shearson-Hammill was worked out with considerable care, and apparently with help from the inside. According to a complaint signed by Sgt. Thomas Dolan of the Manhattan South Detective Squad and on file in the Manhattan Criminal Court, here's how the suspects tried to pull off the caper:

Shearson-Hammill in July 1969 received a letter that looked as if it came from a Detroit-area customer, an engineering firm, directing the brokerage firm to transfer $740,000 of the customer's Treasury bills to the New York office of Swiss Bank Corp.

The letter looked legitimate. It listed the correct amount of the Treasury bills and bore the names of the top officers of Shearson-Hammill's corporate customer. But, the complaint says, the names of the officers were forged.

A few days before the letter was received, a 27-year-old New Yorker named Marvin Sperling appeared at the Swiss bank's New York office, identified himself as Anthony M. Sabatello, and said he intended to open an account in the bank's Zurich office.

The next day, Mr. Sperling flew to Zurich. With him went another 27-year-old New Yorker, Vincent Gullo, "to ensure that Sperling shared the wrongfully obtained money with Gullo and his other accomplices," according to the complaint.

They registered at a Hilton hotel in Zurich. Mr. Sperling then opened an account at the bank under the name of Anthony M. Sabatello. After this, Mr. Sperling is accused of having a letter prepared, bearing the signature of Anthony M. Sabatello, directing the Swiss bank to take possession of the Treasury bills from Shearson-Hammill, sell them and send the proceeds to the Sabatello account in Zurich, according to the complaint.

The money never was collected. Mr. Sperling and Mr. Gullo were subsequently arrested in New York, accused of attempted grand larceny, forgery and conspiracy. Mr. Sperling was released on his own recognizance; Mr. Gullo was freed on $5,000 bail. A court hearing is scheduled to determine if a crime has been committed and if there are reasonable grounds to believe Mr. Sperling and Mr. Gullo committed the crime.

Why didn't the alleged scheme work? Shearson-Hammill didn't transfer the Treasury bills to the Swiss bank's New York office. Though the brokerage firm received an allegedly forged letter in the name of its Detroit customer, the Swiss bank didn't receive any such letter in the name of the Detroit customer to alert the bank to expect the Treasury bills from Shearson-Hammill. Learning that no such letter had been received by the bank, Shearson-Hammill checked back with the customer and discovered that it hadn't ordered any transfer of funds.

Smith & Wesson's Mr. Barry says organized criminal gangs are responsible for many of the stock thefts in recent years. Often, he says, these gangs receive help from an employe inside the brokerage firm. "In many cases, a clerk has a gambling problem, or narcotics problem, and this makes him susceptible to criminal elements," Mr. Barry says.

In countering the problem, the brokerage firms are getting smarter themselves. They are tightening their auditing controls to make it easier to catch false entries and spot bogus letters. A few firms require that workers be willing to take a lie detector test as a condition of employment. A recent law passed in New York State requiring fingerprinting of employes of brokerage firms belonging to national exchanges gives the firms a tool to weed out suspects in sensitive posts.

Will all those measures eliminate stock thefts? At least one broker doubts it.

"I don't think you'll eliminate theft till you eliminate the stock certificate," says a source at Walston & Co., which last year suffered the disappearance of some securities from the firm.

But even the end of the certificate may not thwart the sophisticated crook.

—STANLEY PENN

Buy Now, Pay Never

MACK and Louie used to make a total of nearly $100,-000 a year, which isn't bad for a couple of bartenders, even in New York. Mack and Louie were friendly to their patrons, business was good and tips were often generous.

But police say Mack and Louie had a little something extra going for them—simple but profitable. According to police, the two would purchase stolen credit cards, use the cards to buy airline tickets and sell the tickets at cut rates to customers of the midtown Manhattan bar where they worked. Then they would pocket the money.

Because the police were tipped off, the life style of Mack and Louie has changed recently. They have been arrested and now are awaiting trial. But the lucrative scheme illustrates a point: Thefts of credit cards, long a major problem, are rising more rapidly than ever, and causing real trouble for the banks, department stores, oil firms and other companies that issue the cards.

No one knows for sure how much money businesses are losing because of credit-card thefts. But Standard Oil Co. of Ohio, which surveyed 15 major oil concerns, found that stolen cards cost those firms nearly $23 million in 1969, up from $14 million in 1968.

"Credit-card fraud is reaching epidemic proportions," says H. B. Loomis, director of security for Ohio Standard. "We're launching an all-out war against it." To combat credit-card thieves, Sohio has set up a special task force, which has helped make an average of one arrest every three days.

In Washington, D.C., Riggs National Bank says its Central Charge Service lost over $1 million in the first nine months of 1970 from "large-scale theft of cards." The loss for all 1969 was "substantially less," the bank says. And a loss of $700,000 in 1969 from such thefts, more than double two years previously, was registered by Federated Department Stores, which owns among other stores Filene's in New England, I. Magnin in San Francisco and Boston Store in Milwaukee.

Banks and retailers that issue cards are usually stuck with the greater portion of such losses. They generally don't attempt to hold the original owner of the card liable after it is stolen—at least not beyond a stated, relatively small amount and provided, in some cases, that the owner gives notification of the theft within a certain period. The competition among issuers of cards has forced them to eliminate or hold down any liability on the owner's part. Some states also have laws limiting the owner's liability.

One factor underlying the growing theft problem is the soaring number of credit cards in circulation. Holders of BankAmericards, for example, now number 31.6 million, nearly double the 16.7 million of 1968. Currently there are 300 million credit cards in this country, or better than one for every man, woman and child, estimates Eugene Gold, district attorney in New York's borough of Brooklyn, who has prosecuted about 50 cases of credit-card fraud.

Thieves get the cards in a variety of ways. Sometimes cards are stolen from home and street mailboxes;

this was especially so when issuers mailed out masses of cards in brightly colored envelopes that were easy to spot, police officers say. But mass mailings were all but eliminated recently when the Federal Trade Commission barred the mailing of unsolicited cards. The FTC's step was aimed, in part, at reducing card thefts.

In the case of Mack and Louie in New York, the story often began with a businessman's visit to a prostitute, police say. A pimp or the prostitute would steal the man's credit cards and later sell them to Mack. The bartender would also buy stolen cards from pickpockets and other petty thieves.

Once Mack had enough cards, he and Louie would ask customers at the bar where they would like to travel, police say. Would the junior executive like to go to Chicago? Maybe Los Angeles? Or Las Vegas perhaps? The friendly bartenders would then visit an airline office, use one of their stolen credit cards to buy the ticket and sell it to the traveler at half price, the New York police allege.

Some credit-card thieves are hooked up with the Mafia, authorities say. Brooklyn's Mr. Gold says half of the 50 cases he has prosecuted have involved organized crime. "Credit-card fraud isn't a major business for organized crime, like loan sharking is, but professional criminals are using the cards to get around the country free," Mr. Gold says.

One case began in a small Kentucky town on July 9, 1970, when an executive was mugged and robbed of his Diners' Club credit card. By August the card had apparently found its way into the hands of the Mafia in Pittsburgh.

A lodger at the Hospitality Motor Inn in Pittsburgh attracted the attention of a desk clerk, who said later he felt the man was "suspicious-looking." The clerk's curiosity was further aroused when another man paid part of the lodger's bill. The clerk called hotel security officers, who found that the stolen Diners' Club card had been used by the second man to pay the bill. Armed with this information, the officers had the two men arrested when they returned to the hotel.

The lodger turned out to be a reputed top lieutenant in the Mafia. The man who had paid the bill with the stolen credit card was one of his henchmen. Besides the Diners' Club card, the henchman was also carrying stolen American Express, Carte Blanche, Gulf Oil, Phillips 66 and Playboy Club cards, two BankAmericards and a Charge Association of Cincinnati card. Subsequent checks showed that purchases just for airline tickets on one of the cards totaled $9,800.

For lack of evidence, charges were dropped against the reputed Mafia lieutenant, who carried none of the cards. But the henchman was charged with forgery, receiving stolen goods and illegal use of credit cards. The case is pending.

From a criminal's point of view, the best way to obtain credit cards is not to steal them himself but to get them from a dishonest employe within a credit-card organization. The dishonest employe can supply the cards in quantity and can provide them before they have been signed by the individuals for whom they are intended.

In one case, a New York ring of six criminals paid an employe of a bank-card association to steal Master Charge cards. Before he was caught, the employe provided about 50 unsigned cards. A tip to New York police broke up the ring. Some members were convicted of fraud charges, others pleaded guilty and still others are yet to be tried.

The New York group had a variety of wares for sale. For $50 you could buy an American Express card, which the rightful owner had signed; for $100 you could buy an unsigned Master Charge card. And then there was a $500 package deal. It consisted of one American Express card, one Master Charge, two oil-company cards and one forged driver's license, all conveniently issued to the same name.

In the black market dealing in stolen cards, the most valuable of all are so-called "Q" cards, police officers say. These are cards that are issued to companies rather than individuals and that may legitimately be used by anyone in the company. Such cards are especially valuable to thieves because the bearer of a "Q" card need not present any other identification. These cards bring "about $2,000 each" in the black market, one assistant district attorney says.

Some users of stolen credit cards find they can't buy what they want with the cards they have. So they use the cards to purchase goods readily convertible into cash. Such a technique, police charge, was used by black militants in Pittsburgh seeking to finance a "revolution." The group fraudulently obtained about 30 credit cards and went on a buying binge, purchasing up to $75,000 in cameras, electric frying pans and motion-picture projectors, police say. Members also rented Hertz and Avis cars and drove them into auto shops to buy tires and batteries, the police say.

The militants then allegedly held a sale for friends and acquaintances, offering such bargains as $150 cameras and $50 tires at half-price. Authorities charge that the militants were in the midst of using the proceeds to buy guns and ammunition when they were caught by police and security representatives of Ohio Standard. Charges against the individual members are still pending.

A cooperating merchant can be a great help to

those who fradulently use credit cards. The militants in Pittsburgh, besides their cut-rate sales, raised cash by working with a dealer in second-hand cars, police charge. The militants would borrow a used car from the dealer's lot, take it out and buy new tires and batteries for it, "maybe have some body work done and get it really spruced up," an investigator says. They would use their credit cards to pay for the work, of course. Then they would return the car to the dealer, who could get a much higher price for the reconditioned auto. The militants and the dealer would split the profits from the higher price, the investigator says.

In a Boston case, a credit-card thief "bought" items from a cooperating gas-station manager, although the thief never actually took the goods. When a local bank reimbursed the manager for the items charged on the credit card, he and the thief split the cash.

To try to block the increasing misuse of credit cards, banks, oil companies and other card issuers are taking a number of steps, some of which they and police won't discuss. When bank-card associations mail cards, they now often send them by registered mail and usually stagger the mailings. "We've also stopped using bright orange envelopes marked, 'valuable credit card inside,' " says a Master Charge official.

In general, retailers are supposed to telephone credit-card associations when a cardholder's purchase exceeds a specified amount. The associations then confirm that the holder's credit is good and that the card isn't stolen. But, in the past, when the limit never changed, thieves would buy items just under the specified price.

Now some groups of card issuers are varying the figure. The New England Bankcard Association changes the figure on a random basis, for instance. While most stores might check on any purchase over $50, during one week all retailers on one street might inquire about those over $20. Or all hardware stores in the area might check on purchases over $30 for three weeks.

Other card issuers have gone along with Ohio Standard in setting up special task forces to combat misuse of cards. At Sohio, the force comprises former FBI men and detectives, who have helped begin 93 prosecutions. Of these, 58 convictions have resulted, charges have been dropped in one case and 34 others are pending.

—Liz Roman Gallese

Auto Theft Pros

A LFRED, a 40-year-old florist, had his heart set on a "trumpet gold" 1969 Buick Electra, but he couldn't afford one until a friend of a friend told him how.

"It's easy," the man whispered. "First, you give me $1,000, and I'll sell you a stolen, used Mustang. I'll resteal it, and you'll collect $2,000 from your insurance company. With the $2,000, you buy a stolen Cadillac Coupe de Ville from me. I'll resteal it, and you'll collect $5,000 on the insurance. Then you can go to a legitimate auto dealer and buy the Buick."

Alfred got the car of his dreams through the scheme, but he also got caught in a New York police investigation of organized auto theft rings and currently faces prosecution for insurance fraud and receiving stolen property. However, police here and elsewhere admit that they don't apprehend nearly enough Alfreds or their suppliers.

In recent years, auto theft has risen faster than any other U.S. crime category. The National Automobile Theft Bureau (NATB), the investigating arm of 400 insurance companies, estimates that $800 million worth of cars were stolen in this country in 1968, 22% more than in 1967 and double the amount just five years before.

Even more alarming to law enforcement officials

is evidence that the crime increasingly is becoming the province of gangs of professional thieves. Most auto thefts still are perpetrated by youths under 21 years of age, who use the vehicles for "joy rides" and abandon them within a day or so. But Federal Bureau of Investigation statistics show that the proportion of stolen cars that aren't recovered—the mark of the professional thief—is on the increase. That figure rose to 17% of the 800,000 cars stolen in 1968, up from 15% in 1967 and 10% in 1966. In New York, a prime target for professional rings, fully 36% of the autos stolen in 1968 still were missing by early 1969.

The impact of this development extends beyond the direct victims of the thieves. "The increasing participation of hardened criminals in taking cars, and the finesse with which they pass them on to buyers, is boosting auto insurance rates for every driver," says Thomas J. Mackell, district attorney for the borough of Queens in New York. Arrests made by detectives working with Dist. Atty. Mackell were credited with exposing two auto theft rings in New York last year.

Police estimate that some 300 professional car theft gangs are active around the country. They say that the methods of most of these rings bear little resemblance to those of pre-World War II days, when auto thieves concentrated on inconspicuous, medium-priced autos and maintained clandestine body shops to alter the car's appearance before attempting to sell them.

The organized rings now at work deal mainly in high-priced cars such as Cadillacs, Chevrolet Corvettes and Ford Thunderbirds. Demand for expensive autos is high, and on today's crowded streets they aren't as conspicuous as they once were. Moreover, the pros rarely alter the appearance of cars they steal. The tampering that's done to throw police off the track is limited to the complex auto license and registration papers that states require.

By manipulating auto registration papers to avoid detection, professional thieves can steal the same car more than once. Anthony DeStasio, special agent in New York for the NATB, says that one 1967 Cadillac was stolen seven times before it wound up in police hands. The thieves made a profit of about $20,000 on the various transactions, he says. In each case, the buyer was "in" on the deal, and was allowed to keep the car long enough to qualify for the insurance payment for his subsequent "loss."

Police officials agree that auto theft gangs couldn't operate without the connivance of their customers, who must be willing to take some risk for the "bargain" car prices they get. Convictions for receiving stolen merchandise are rare because it must be proved that the recipient knew the goods were stolen, but anyone who buys a stolen car (or anything else) can have it taken away from him without compensation if police find it in his possession.

Most buyers of "hot" cars are middle-income people with no criminal records, says Robert Sadowski, deputy chief of the Queens district attorney's rackets bureau. "But they have larceny in their hearts—they want something for nothing," he asserts. He notes that the two rings uncovered in Queens in 1968 were selling Cadillacs worth $6,000 for about $2,500.

Irving B. Guller, associate professor of psychology at John Jay College of Criminal Law in New York, says that middle-class people seem increasingly willing to go along with such schemes because of "the growing publicity about how rich people make it by skirting the law." He continues: "To a lot of people, owning a Caddy amounts to 'making it,' and there's a growing belief that once you make it no one will care how."

Police say that auto theft pros often make use of persons who don't otherwise engage in criminal activity. "It's the friend-of-a-friend thing," says one New York auto squad detective. "Someone in a gang will tell a relative or a bartender or someone that a great car deal is available and to pass it on if they know anyone who might be interested. Sometimes, these middle-men get a little commission for a sale."

Cars stolen in this country sometimes end up in the hands of foreign buyers who are outside the reach of U.S. law. Police say that in a matter of hours a car stolen off the streets of New York or some other American port city can be aboard a ship leaving the country. These autos rarely are recovered because shippers and U.S. customs agents aren't required to verify the ownership of goods headed out of the U.S., and customs officials in the countries of destination don't have time to check the papers accompanying the autos through the labyrinth of American police files.

No one knows how many stolen cars leave the U.S. each year, but the number is substantial. Thomas F. Jones, chief investigator for the New York Harbor Waterfront Commission, says his men recently took the shipping documents of 4,800 cars that left the U.S. in the summer of 1968 and checked them against FBI stolen car reports. They found that more than 100 of the cars had been stolen.

Donald Armstrong, manager of the NATB's Eastern division, says police have traced stolen American cars to an Arabian sheik, several exiled Argentinian government officials and the police chief of a Latin American city.

Professional car thieves owe much of their success

to their skill in procuring the papers needed to establish ownership to the vehicles they steal. Police say that many stolen cars are supplied with papers from New York or Massachusetts, which, unlike most states, don't require motorists to have title papers to prove vehicle ownership once they've been issued a state registration certificate.

Massachusetts is a favorite hunting ground for thieves in search of auto ownership documents. State law there requires motorists to have their registration certificates with them while driving, and many car owners comply by leaving their certificates in their glove compartments—a tempting target for thieves.

One professional car theft ring recently uncovered in New York utilized stolen Massachusetts registration papers for cars stolen in New York. According to New York police, members of the ring took regular trips to Boston, where they stole auto registration certificates and vehicle identification tags—the coded numbers usually found on car door posts—from vehicles parked in airport, motel and restaurant parking lots. They concentrated on the high-priced, late-model cars they knew their customers would want.

The ring took the Massachusetts auto ownership documents to New York. Using fictitious names under which they had previously obtained phony drivers' licenses and other identification, they presented the stolen car ownership papers at the New York Motor Vehicle Bureau. Stating they had purchased the cars in question from their Massachusetts owners, they received bona fide New York registration certificates and license plates. Even if Massachusetts authorities sought to trace the stolen registration documents, they would have been thwarted by New York procedures that make it hard to link vehicle identification numbers with the cars' new owners, police say.

The thieves then proceeded to search New York streets for cars that matched the registration documents. Once they had spotted and broken into a car, they would quickly remove its vehicle identification tag and replace it with one stolen from a Massachusetts car, for which they had matching ownership papers. The car, with the correct papers, would be driven off for delivery to a waiting buyer.

"Within five minutes, the thief would drive away with the stolen car, and any policeman happening to stop him would have no way of quickly proving the car wasn't his," says George Rapp, a detective with the New York police auto theft squad.

The ring was broken only with the help of a tipster, police say.

Another ring that New York police claim to have broken with a number of arrests got its ownership documents by stealing forms that auto dealers use to obtain registration certificates for cars in their possession. Presenting large numbers of these forms in numbered sequence might have aroused the suspicions of the state's Motor Vehicle Bureau, so the gang bribed three employes of the bureau to process their applications, police say.

"The operation of this outfit was so refined that a customer who placed an order for a specific car at 9 a.m. could get delivery, with all the necessary papers, by 11 a.m.," says Peter Pawlyk, an auto theft squad detective.

Law enforcement agencies agree that any substantial success in fighting organized auto thieves depends on the establishment of a central computer facility to combine motor vehicle registration data from all 50 states. Present variations in state auto registration law and data processing practices give thieves too much room to maneuver, they assert. For instance, police say that some car theft gangs started obtaining auto ownership documents in Rhode Island after the recent discovery of the gang that operated in Massachusetts. Rhode Island also doesn't require car owners to have title papers once they've been issued a state registration certificate.

Auto makers have moved to make it more difficult for their cars to be broken into. U.S. manufacturers in recent years have begun installing more complex door locks that are harder for thieves to open than previous models. Starting with its 1969 cars, General Motors autos have a device that locks the steering wheel in place when the ignition key is removed. Ford, Chrysler and American Motors have similar locks on 1970 models.

Manufacturers also are experimenting with ways to make it tougher for thieves to start cars by "jumping" ignition cables.

But police who specialize in investigating auto thefts express skepticism that such methods will work for very long. Stories of the mechanical inventiveness of professional car thieves abound in many police departments. New York police say that one man who was convicted of car theft was found strolling around the corridors of his cell block shortly after he was imprisoned. He had found a way to pick a lock on his cell door—which supposedly required a complicated, six-inch-long key to open.

—LEE BERTON

The VW Caper

A GROWING band of dedicated men in Southern California have devoted themselves to making the squat, ugly Volkswagen into an automotive sex symbol —the gaudy, rakish dune buggy.

These men are thieves.

Not everyone who converts a pedestrian Volkswagen into a glossy, fat-tired dune buggy is a thief, of course. But many of the face-lifters are crooks, and, judging by the number of Volkswagens being spirited away and the concurrent wailing of insurance companies, their numbers are multiplying. The problem isn't peculiar to Southern California—dune buggies are spreading wherever there is sand and some places where there isn't, and the thieves are following right along.

But it is in the land of sun and sand that the rape of the Love Bug and its metamorphosis into a Mexican Chrome Splash Special or Terra-Tired Sand Pounder has become something of a cottage industry. One reason: An abundance of raw material. About 65,000 VWs a year are sold in the area, making it one of Volkswagen's prime U.S. markets.

The bug is prized for its lightweight, tough, economical engine, considered perfect for dune buggy use. The most ornate buggies may sport enormous racing tires, high-performance cams, mag wheels, jet air scoops, leather bucket seats and other extravagant extras that can cost as much as $3,000. But underneath all the glitter there usually sits a simple, sturdy Volkswagen engine, drive train and chassis.

The dune buggy craze has in fact all but wiped certain used VW parts off the open market, and a thriving black market in stolen parts has sprung up to fill the need. In Los Angeles, the Beetle has shot past Ford and now trails only Chevrolet as the most-stolen car, and the police department has named one of its sergeants a specialist in recovery of stolen and converted VWs.

When those victimized by VW thieves do manage to get their cars back, they often wish they hadn't. Leonard Baruch, a Los Angeles college student, one day found an empty space where his 1966 VW had been. He wrote the car off as gone forever and with his insurance money sadly bought a Chevy. Ten months later police found the VW. Leonard took one look at his once-sedate beetle—now a low-slung, sawed-off bomb with a gold flake paint job that hurt the eyes—and gladly fled to his Chevy.

If thieves don't convert a stolen VW, they're likely to use it as a parts depot to peddle cheap components to innocents building their own dune buggies. When one young New Yorker recently reported his 1967 VW stolen, the cops found it in a matter of days—sitting forlornly in a Union City, N.J., vacant lot, minus seats, bumpers, radio, battery and several parts of the engine.

Anguished insurance men say those two VW owners were lucky to even learn of the fate of their bugs. It is not just that the incidence of VW thefts has grown "by leaps and bounds," they say; the rate of "total loss" on such thefts runs close to 95%, compared with 20% on American cars.

Losses would be even greater if it weren't for men

like Sgt. Ted Breckenridge, the Los Angeles cop assigned to tracking down stolen VWs. Sgt. Breckenridge spends much time prowling about dune buggy rallies in disguise—sport shirt, baggy pants, scuffed shoes—looking for the remains of hot beetles. It was he who tracked down the notorious Moretti-Rowe gang, a group whose enthusiasm for Grand Theft, Auto, was matched only by its awesome ineptitude in carrying the crime off cleanly.

The Moretti-Rowe gang members—namely Moretti and Rowe—are now guests of the state, but at the height of their practice they were busy men indeed—so busy they were easy to track. Wherever they went, Sgt. Breckenridge recalls, Frank Rowe and Willie Moretti trailed a string of VW shells, dented husks bereft of insides. The sergeant says he found stripped VWs "all over the San Fernando Valley—on the roadside, in alleys, carports, walnut groves, all over the place."

Frank Rowe, possessor of a ducktail haircut and a deep conviction that he was a mechanical wizard, did most of the VW work—stripping off the bodies, altering the chassis, adding fiber glass shells, and advertising and selling the finished product. But in truth, police say, Frank was a bumbler as a thief and worse as a mechanic. Not only was his handiwork readily identifiable to Sgt. Breckenridge, who arrested him six times, but his customers were less than happy with the botched-up buggies Frank delivered to them—vehicles with shock absorbers installed upside down, parts improperly welded and floor pans riddled with holes.

Frank's work deteriorated still more when he somehow convinced himself that his lawman foe was tracking him down by his welding technique. So, says the sergeant, Frank decided "to switch and weld with his left hand so he wouldn't leave a recognizable pattern."

Frank's sidekick, Willie Moretti, was a specialist in the marketing of hot Porsches. But an escape artist he was not. When police put out a warrant for his arrest, Willie swiped a light plane from Van Nuys Airport and headed for Mexico; he was almost there before he realized he didn't know how to land the plane, so he smashed it into the ground and strolled away unscathed—into the waiting arms of the police.

Inept Willie and Frank may have been, but not so inept that they didn't manage to filch some 300 cars, mostly VWs, before being locked away. Other gangs, as well as countless lone-wolf entrepreneurs, take a similar toll, and Horst Entholt, service manager for Volkswagen Pacific, the company's West Coast distributor, says that Volkswagenwerk A.G. back at the factory in Germany, "is working on the problem feverishly."

Thus, new additions to 1971 VWs include steering wheel locks and a more thief-proof wing window as standard, and a lockable gearshift, a front hood lock and an engine compartment lock as optional. Nonetheless, insurance men, police and VW executives all agree that people will be trying to steal beetles by the thousands as long as the dune buggy fad continues—and that fad seems to have a lot of steam left.

It may be that the insurance men are not optimistic because they are aware of the way the lust for a dune buggy can possess a man. An insurance claims adjuster in Orange County, Calif., says his supervisor keeps hounding him for tips on where to find salvaged beetles. "He wants one to make into a buggy," says the adjuster.

"But," he adds, "I don't tell him when I find one. I don't like him."

—G. Christian Hill

Highway Robbery

IT'S spring, and the Easter hijacking season is at hand.

That means it's especially dangerous to send trucks full of apparel over the nation's highways. For hijacking has some seasonal factors, and at the moment the demand is for new finery for the Easter Parade. As Mother's Day approaches, the demand will be for appliances. Typewriters will be in big demand as schools prepare to reopen in the fall, and liquor trucks are always in special peril around Christmastime.

That's how sophisticated the truck hijacking business has become. No longer is hijacking just a minor threat posed by minor criminals. Now it is a well organized big business—nearly three quarters of a billion dollars worth of goods were stolen in transit last year, according to one estimate—and it is being run by professional thieves, some of whom seem to have Mafia connections.

The value of goods stolen in 1969 was 17% higher than the 1968 total, which alarms truckers and law enforcement officials alike. Even more alarming, however, is that in four of every five hijackings the cargo is not recovered and the thieves aren't apprehended. Victims and law officials say that about the only comforting fact is that the hijackers seldom resort to violence.

Officials say hijacking is on the increase for several reasons. There are more trucks around to be hijacked. Also, shippers increasingly are loading trucks full of a single product, which attracts hijackers who don't want to have to bother disposing of several different types of commodities. Authorities further note that there is more of a market for stolen goods as bargain-hunting consumers and financially pressed small retailers seek out their neighborhood "fences"—shady operators who buy stolen goods. And finally, it is relatively easy to steal trucks, which often are left unguarded.

The sharp growth in hijackings clearly alarms shippers and Federal and local police officials. Hijacking an interstate shipment of goods already is a Federal crime punishable by up to 10 years in prison, but there is some feeling in Washington that the penalty is not harsh enough. As truckers suffer ever-larger losses to hijackers they are being forced to pay ever-larger insurance premiums. One insurance official says rates have gone up 15% to 25% recently, with the trucker himself having to pay for an increasing share of the loss—now as much as 50%. "Many truckers are having trouble getting cargo insurance" at any rate, says an insurer.

To try to stem their losses, the truckers are devising all sorts of security schemes, ranging from two-way radio systems to armed guards. They also are seeking to check thoroughly the background of those applying for work in an effort to halt the number of inside jobs. While there's no official national estimate of how many thefts are carried out with the aid of a driver or dispatcher, one New York detective who heads a squad pursuing the offenders claims it amounts to 60%.

But the security methods often don't work too well.

In one instance, two drivers, who had two-way radios in their trucks, decided as a further precaution to stick together on the road. That way, if one encountered armed robbers and couldn't radio for help, his buddy could. During the trip, the two drivers stopped for coffee. When they came back to their trucks, they were met by five armed men. Two of the robbers made off with the trucks while the other three took the drivers for a three-hour ride. The drivers called the police when they were released.

Police later found one of the trucks, still loaded with its $125,000 worth of cigarets, in a turnpike service area. The truck engine had failed. The FBI soon learned from a paid informer that one of the drivers had arranged the hijacking to settle a $5,000 gambling debt. In all, the FBI arrested 12 men, including the driver, and recovered most of the cigarets.

Even when a hijacker is arrested, it's often a long time before he is imprisoned. After five trials (there were hung juries, mistrials and other problems), four reputed Mafia members were sentenced in June 1969 for a $15,000 textile hijacking 10 years earlier. The men are free on bail pending their appeal.

Because hijacking is relatively risk-free, it is said to appeal to the Mafia more than bank robbing. Indeed, the take from hijackings in 1969 was 70 to 75 times the $10 million stolen from banks in 1968, the latest year for which bank figures are available.

The one in five hijackers who is caught is usually arrested as a result of a tip from a paid informer. The FBI is known to pay thousands of dollars for useful information.

Still, old-fashioned police sleuthing also helps. For example, a truck containing $200,000 worth of mercury was stolen on New York's Staten Island not so long ago.

When the abandoned truck was found, lawmen noted that only five miles had been registered on the odometer after the hijacking. So they covered an area within a five-mile radius and soon found the mercury at a scrap dealer's. Two men have been indicted and await trial.

Some other hijackings have gone awry even before the goods were unloaded. Sometimes the hijackers steal the wrong truck. At least two trucks have been abandoned with the goods intact because the hijackers apparently had stolen the wrong vehicles. One truck contained frozen pizzas. The other contained a trailerload of size 44 bras.

—John D. Williams

Safer Skies

IN Atlanta's airport, a young couple dressed in wild "mod" attire and carrying a loudly blaring radio looked like just another part of the Now Generation. But as the two prepared to board an Eastern Air Lines flight bound for Newark, the airline found their behavior suspicious. It's glad it did.

The two weren't willing to pass through a newly installed metal detecting device. When asked for identification, they produced impressive credit cards—inscribed with a variety of names. The airline then had them searched by a U.S. marshal. He found the "woman" was carrying a loaded .38 caliber pistol and 20 rounds of ammunition. She was also found to be a man in disguise. The two were arrested and the flight was made safely.

The arrests mark a real change. Not long ago, the two travelers could probably have boarded their flight with no questions asked. From late 1967 to late 1969, Eastern had 19 of its planes hijacked. But in the following year—after it stepped up security efforts—only one Eastern plane was hijacked.

Eastern isn't alone in curbing hijackings. Though Middle East "skyjackings" have terrified travelers and again dramatized the problem, the actual number of U.S. airline hijackings has declined significantly. In the first 10 months of 1970, 15 American aircraft were diverted, down sharply from a record 33 in 1969 and from 26 the previous year. For instance, National Airlines, which had been only slightly less troubled than Eastern, experienced only one hijacking in the first 10 months of 1970, a drop from eight last year.

Airline efforts to tighten security have caught numerous would-be hijackers and clearly deterred countless others, aviation officials say. "Now potential hijackers know they run a substantial risk of being discovered before they board the airliner," one Eastern executive notes. He says "quite a few" discarded guns have been found near boarding areas, a fact he attributes to the deterrent effect of security measures.

To be sure, the number of American planes diverted to places other than Cuba has risen a bit. This complicates the problem because new destinations imply new objectives and different types of criminals. For instance, hijackers with political motives like the Palestinian guerrillas are often sophisticated in their planning. They work in groups more often than the typical Havana-bound skyjackers.

And of course some hijackers are still getting through the tightened security. "We don't have the capability right now of being foolproof," concedes a Trans World Airlines official.

The task of detecting hijackers is enormous. Eastern alone carries more than 22 million passengers on 511,000 flights a year. But since the carrier started its antihijack program, it has denied passage to 55 people and 17 of these were arrested. The carrying of concealed weapons or illegal drugs prompted most of the arrests. (The others denied passage acted in a highly suspicious manner and typically refused to be searched but didn't actually break laws.)

"We're looking for the needle in the haystack and so far I'd say we've found 17 needles," says Jack Shields, Eastern's manager of operational safety.

All major airlines have started antihijack programs. Eastern's was the first. The carrier estimates it has spent about $1 million in equipment and training for the program. It says the figure would be considerably higher if the cost of flight delays caused by security measures were included.

New measures are rapidly being developed, but at present U.S. airlines rely basically on two methods of hijack prevention. These are the judging of passengers against the Federal Aviation Administration's "hijacker behavior profile" and use of a metal detector called the magnetometer.

Both measures are used on the ground. While armed guards are increasingly placed on flights, most airlines and aviation experts think it is vital to stop the potential skyjacker early. "We've decided the best place to stop these hijackings is on the ground," says an FAA spokesman.

The behavior pattern is based on the conduct of past hijackers. The pattern is confidential, but it is known, for instance, that the less sophisticated type of conspirator often buys a one-way ticket. Hijackers are often noticeably nervous, too. "Anybody who's about to hijack a plane has got to be nervous," notes Vincent Catania, an Eastern boarding supervisor at New York's Kennedy Airport.

The profile shows that hijackers don't always fit the popular stereotype; the airborne criminal may be a quiet individual in a three-piece suit as well as a wild-eyed fanatic. Moreover, the profile is always changing. For instance, hijackers increasingly work in groups.

But the profile has drawbacks. As it was based mainly on Cuba-bound hijackers, its scope is limited. Used mainly to alert airlines and help them spot passengers who need further watching, it principally complements electronic devices.

The main electronic gadget in use is the magnetometer, which measures the amount of iron and steel in baggage and on passengers. Passengers walk between two seven-foot metallic poles. In one form or another, this relatively simple device has been used for about 50 years, mainly to detect weapons on prison inmates. But these days the old gadget is in hot demand. Infinetics Inc., a Wilmington, Del., firm that is the biggest maker of magnetometers for airline use, says it has sold more than 200 of the devices to over 20 domestic and overseas carriers. Each instrument costs $968.

The principal drawback is that the magnetometer registers significant amounts of metal for nearly 60% of all passengers. The metal object usually turns out to be a tape recorder or camera. But when the magnetometer is used in conjunction with the hijacker behavior profile, only about 1% of all passengers are interrogated and searched, says an FAA official.

Airlines say the magnetometer-profile system does produce results. "To this date there has never been a hijacking where we've had the system in operation," says Eastern's Mr. Shields.

But airlines and FAA officials generally agree that improvements will be necessary. Westinghouse Electric Corp. is completing development of an "active electromagnetic device" which the company claims "can discriminate between guns and other common metal bearing objects."

The device differentiates between the magnetic impulses of a gun and those of other objects; this should reduce the number of false alarms caused by existing magnetometers, Westinghouse claims. Besides causing delays, false alarms divert attention from authentic conspirators, of course.

Bendix Corp. is currently perfecting an X-Ray device that can detect a gun or knife on a person's body. The weapon appears on a television screen as a dark shadow within a lighter image of the individual; it stays on the screen for up to two minutes while the image is studied.

The instrument emits a dosage only 1-400 the strength of a chest X-ray, the company says. Unlike more powerful X-rays, it thus wouldn't harm photographic film, Bendix claims. The main problem in using the device might come when, say, 200 or more passengers must be examined individually and time is of the essence, says David Ebeoglu, a nuclear physicist at Bendix.

Other companies are working on the problem, too. The FAA estimates it has received over 200 inquiries from companies interested in developing more sophisticated gadgets to stop hijackers.

But it isn't only tightened airline security that is curbing hijackings. Cuba recently sent one hijacker back to the United States to face trial here. Some hijackers unhappy with their lot in Cuba, have voluntarily returned to trial here, and some prison sentences to hijackers have been stiff. These factors are significant deterrents, airlines believe.

And, of course, even though antihijack devices improve there is still human error. At Newark, N.J. Airport one evening, an Eastern ticket agent spotted a young Tampa-bound passenger who seemed to fit the hijacker profile. The magnetometer showed a significant amount of metal on the man, and law enforcement officials were quickly summoned.

But while police and airline personnel busily questioned and searched the young man—who turned out to be unarmed—a young Cuban named Daniel Lopez and his family walked through an adjacent gate. Though they slipped through practically unnoticed, they were carrying a gun, a homemade bomb, several bottles of gasoline and a bayonet. Before long, the Miami-bound plane was a Havana-bound plane.

—DAVID GUMPERT

Hard Travelin'

I STOLE a suitcase the other day.

I did it to confirm that it's a snap to heist luggage from an airport baggage claim area. Like a professional baggage thief, I waited until most passengers arriving on a Delta Air Lines flight from Atlanta had picked their bags off the revolving merry-go-round machine that receives bags from the conveyor belt at San Francisco International Airport.

When I spotted one still going around with no apparent owner nearby, I strolled over, took it and walked casually out of the terminal and to the taxi stand. No one cared the bag wasn't mine.

Unlike a regular crook, however, I brought the suitcase back, and the owner never knew it had been stolen. He apparently had stopped for a drink and didn't pick his bag up until later. But plenty of other airline passengers never get their bags back. And when they don't, it's the airline that has to pay.

While industry loss figures aren't tabulated, the Air Transport Association made a survey in 1967 that disclosed that during the year carriers had nearly 24,000 "permanently lost" bag claims and shelled out $5.3 million to angry passengers. Since then, the losses have gone up sharply, airlines say.

Trans World Airlines, for example, says it paid out

more than $1 million in claims in 1968, about a 25% gain from the year before. American Airlines says that in August 1969 it paid 287 claims for "lost" bags compared with 275 in the comparable month of 1968, although the airline notes that it handled nearly 200,000 more bags in August 1969.

The result is that in many cities the airlines are hiring guards who make a traveler show his claim check before they let him walk off with a bag. United Air Lines has posted blue-uniformed guards in San Francisco, near the scene of my crime, and they "pay for themselves" in reducing baggage thefts, according to Herman J. Oldigs, United's passenger service supervisor here.

But most baggage areas are big, open spaces, and in some it is still quite easy to get past the guards. The airlines are hesitant about installing tighter security measures, however. "If we make things too tight, by building walls around the areas, for instance, we would force people to stand in line to get clear of the guards," says a passenger representative for one airline. And that would create ill will and perhaps cause travelers to switch to other lines, he adds.

Most travelers are well aware of the theft problem, but many still stop off in an airport bar or a restaurant before going to get their bags, which leaves the thief plenty of time to steal a suitcase undetected. Others send their bags ahead of time, or schedule connections so close that their bags miss the planes. In each case, the suitcases are likely to sit around unattended for a time at the destination.

The airlines have become so accustomed to passenger complaints about stolen baggage that many airline workers just automatically reach for a stolen-bag form when they see a worried traveler approach. When I told the Delta representative in San Francisco that a passerby had stolen a suitcase, he just shrugged and said, "It happens all the time."

The Government says an airline is legally liable for up to $500 if a passenger reports one or more bags missing from a domestic flight. The lines willingly and routinely pay the value that the passenger claims on a notarized form, up to the $500 limit. But airlines officials think some passengers try to make a profit on a theft. An inordinately high number of stolen bags contain hand-crafted shoes, Italian silk shirts and tailor-made suits, the suspicious officials say. But they say some passengers quickly scale down their claims when they notice the forms are supplied by the FBI.

Airline officials question passenger honesty in other respects, too. Many suitcases look alike, and passengers sometimes accidentally pick up the wrong bag at the terminal and take it home. "And if the other guy has packed stuff more valuable than yours, maybe you just keep his bag," suggests a cynical airline man.

Other sources say baggage handlers sometimes are the thieves. As many as four different companies might be involved in moving a single piece of luggage at one airport, airline officials say. And during these moves, they say, it is not uncommon for valuables like cameras and liquor to disappear from unlocked bags.

David Bartruff, a photographer in San Anselmo, Calif., will testify to this. He returned from an assignment in Asia recently, and three of his bags cleared customs at Los Angeles and were put on his connecting plane. But the fourth bag, containing a new $210 telephoto lens, never made it. (The airline paid him only $82.90, its legal liability, which on international flights is determined by the weight of the bag.)

Security people say most bags are stolen by organized gangs. San Francisco police not so long ago broke up one ring composed of youths in their late teens who visited the airport almost daily, scattering through arrival lounges and mixing with passengers as they moved to claim areas. After the gang was discovered, police recovered 30 suitcases from a pawn shop that had served as the sales outlet. Police and security officials say the thieves usually have no trouble fencing either the suitcases or the contents, and they say that enough suitcases have cameras or electric razors or other valuables to make the work quite profitable.

—NORMAN SKLAREWITZ

Stealing 101

TO all appearances, Richard S. seems an ordinary Harvard student. A sophomore from the West Coast, his grades are averaging B or better. Recently he joined one of the most respected student activities on campus. He's well liked by classmates.

But Richard is also a thief—and he has no qualms about admitting it to friends.

Several weeks ago, Richard (that isn't his real name) stole an expensive textbook on European history from the Harvard cooperative bookstore. Why? "I needed the book, and they (the store) could afford to lose it," he says blandly.

Richard has joined a small but increasingly troublesome group of collegians: Students who shoplift. They steal books and other merchandise from stores that specialize in campus needs. These light-fingered scholars are fast becoming an enormous problem, spurring school administrators to tighten discipline policies and forcing college stores to take elaborate security measures that make big-city retailers' defenses pale by comparison. Some store operators, complaining of weak-kneed university discipline, are starting to bring criminal charges against the offenders.

So far, Richard hasn't been caught shoplifting, and he indicates he may well steal again. Some of his classmates haven't been as lucky. Nearly 20 Harvard students have been apprehended for stealing from the Harvard co-op—known on campus as the "Coop". Most of the offenders were placed on academic probation but three were suspended from the university—and two of these have already been drafted.

Harvard isn't the only college with problems. Recently 10 undergraduates and 10 graduate students at Yale University have been nabbed for shoplifting at the Yale cooperative store. In California, San Jose State College's Spartan Bookstore is apprehending students at the rate of three or four a week, compared with four a month a year ago. And at the University of Wisconsin cooperative, 95 students have been arrested recently; losses from student theft in the school year are expected to range between $45,000 and $50,000, an official estimates.

Of course, pilferage at all retail outlets—not just college stores—has been climbing for years. But educators find it particularly disheartening that students are involved in such fast-growing numbers. Says Richard C. Carroll, Yale's dean of undergraduate affairs: "It's terribly discouraging that this is flourishing among the intellectual elite, who should know they are risking their careers."

What sort of student shoplifts? Just about anybody is susceptible to the urge to steal, school authorities say. At Harvard, for example, males and females (from neighboring Radcliffe and from Harvard's graduate programs) are proportionately represented among offenders at the "Coop," as are students with high and low grades and undergraduates and grad students. Both Harvard and Yale recently punished divinity students for book thefts, and the University of Colorado bookstore collared a philosophy major attempting to purloin a textbook on ethics.

Talks with university deans, retailers and students indicate that lack of money is rarely a motive for shoplifting. Most offenders have more than enough cash in their pockets to pay for items stolen. Nor are there many out-and-out professionals—students who take hundreds of dollars worth of books over a long period of time to resell.

John Shaw, manager of the University of Wisconsin store, believes that most students consider stealing books from his store a game rather than a crime. "It comes under the heading of sneaking into the movies," he says. "One kid I nailed recently said, 'Are you calling me a thief? All I did was take a book!' "

Harvard junior Jeffrey Alexander, who as a reporter for the Harvard Crimson recently wrote about shoplifting, feels that students he knows are rebelling against the Establishment when they steal. "Everyone feels oppressed by authority—the university administration, the draft boards and so on—and the 'Coop' is the dark side of authority," he says. "Guys feel its prices are outrageous and that it doesn't meet their needs. They take real pride in cheating it."

High-powered merchandising techniques store managers concede, tempt students to steal by enticing them to pick books off the shelves.

Not long ago, the Brigham Young University bookstore in Provo, Utah, modernized its book displays, only to watch in dismay as inventory losses mounted sharply. Similarly, following opening of a new, self-service book section several years ago, losses at the Princeton University cooperative store climbed markedly. "We figured if a self-service store would work anywhere, it would work here in an honor-system school," says Jack Worthington, manager. "But we found we had created a monster."

Sweeping protective measures have since reduced pilferage at the Princeton store. Students now check their briefcases and books outside, and guards stand at the exits. Employes get a $25 reward for tipping management to a shoplifter. Large, wide-angle mirrors are placed about the store to remind shoppers they are being watched.

Most other big college stores are also cracking down. The Harvard "Coop," for example, uses turnstiles at the exits of its book department and hires off-duty city policemen, both plainclothed and in uniform, to patrol the aisles. Students of police administration at San Jose State are paid $2.25 an hour to guard the bookstore there; they aren't at all reluctant to collar their classmates for stealing, a store official says.

Many stores display big signs reading "Shoplifters Will Be Prosecuted." This has drawbacks, though. The bookstore at Texas Technological College, Lubbock, Tex., put up a dozen such signs only to have five stolen within 24 hours.

The grumbling that universities don't deal strongly enough with thieving students is widespread. "The dean usually says it's due to psychological reasons and just slaps the kid on the wrist," gripes Russell L. Reynolds, general manager of the 1,700-member National Association of College Stores. He suggests that the stores take offenders to court.

The University of Colorado has authorized its bookstore to do just that. Previously, accused shoplifters had been disciplined by an administration committee. Roughly 30 students have been arrested recently, however, and the store is confident the harder line is deterring thefts.

The Yale co-op, which has no direct ties with Yale, began turning student shoplifters over to the city police in the mid-1960s after inventory losses reached a record annual rate of $90,000. The store has drawn bitter rebukes from faculty and students for its tough stand, however. After four students were arrested in a few days time, a student member of the co-op's board of directors resigned in protest.

"Distressing as it is, the answer isn't to give students criminal records," maintains Yale's Dean Carroll. Most of the thefts are spontaneous and involve merchandise worth only a few dollars, he says. Moreover, the dean contends some of the shoplifting is inadvertent. He recalls a Yale senior arrested for stealing a $1.65 paperback; during the same visit to the store, however, the student had paid for an $8 book. "It seems logical that had he intended to steal something, he would have taken the more expensive book," Dean Carroll observes.

(In court, the student pleaded nolo contendere—no defense—and received a suspended sentence on a petty theft charge. His offense thus became a matter of record.)

At the height of the controversy in New Haven, Yale administrators convinced co-op officials to relent somewhat on their policy of calling in the police. Now, with the exception of cases of deliberate, premeditated theft (as when a thief brings along a shopping bag to conceal his loot), the store turns students over to the university, which usually places them on some form of probation. Comments co-op manager Charles L. Willoughby: "We have to protect the store, but we also realize our obligation to protect Yale's investment in its students."

Officials at many schools agree that while any sort of student may shoplift, a certain type appears quite frequently. He is "the totally good, totally successful person in high school whose world falls apart in college," according to Harvard psychologist Kenneth T. Dinklage.

He cites an example: A sophomore was caught stealing a book and some pencils from the Harvard store. In tears, he admitted the theft, saying, "I just took the stuff—I don't know why." The youth had been an A student in his small town high school in New Hampshire, captain of the football team and an Eagle Scout. At Harvard, however, he was a C-plus student, had recently broken up with his girl friend and wasn't getting along with his roommates. "The guy was simply hard up for emotional income," says Mr. Dinklage.

The student was required to withdraw from school for a year. He has since returned and hasn't presented any further discipline problems. Indeed, Harvard, along with many other schools, says it rarely if ever sees a repeat shoplifting offender—in marked contrast to petty thieves in the general population, where there is a high rate of repeaters.

Some observers see the rise in college stealing as mirroring a general decline in moral standards. "Students are merely imitating the worst of an immoral society unfolding around them," says Dana L. Farnsworth, director of university health services at Harvard.

Dr. Farnsworth recalls an incident that illustrates his view. The parents of a six-year-old boy received an angry phone call from the father of their son's elementary school seatmate. The irate father complained that their son was continually stealing his son's pencils. "Understand, it's the principle of the thing," he said. "The pencils aren't important. I can get all the pencils I need from the office."

—GLYNN MAPES

The Terrible Williamsons

THE Williamson family, as usual, wintered in Florida. With the coming of spring, they headed north. Awaiting their arrival were many of their long-time acquaintances: Better Business Bureaus, the police and a number of local agencies specializing in consumer fraud.

"We call them the 'Terrible Williamsons,'" says Louis Sisapel, chief investigator for the Better Business Bureau of Metropolitan New York. For the Williamsons, according to Mr. Sisapel, are an itinerant band of men, women and children whose specialty is bilking homeowners with a variety of "home improvement" offers and phony sales pitches.

You say your roof leaks? Or maybe your driveway is cracked or your paint is peeling? Never fear. For a trifling sum, the Williamsons will reseal the roof, resurface the driveway or spray on a new coat of paint. Then they'll take your money and disappear. And before long your roof will leak, your driveway will crack and your paint will peel. "The slickest and most successful clan of bunco, flim-flam confidence artists in the U.S." is the way New York City's Department of Consumer Affairs describes the Williamsons.

Police believe the Williamsons are all descendants and relatives of a canny Scotsman who immigrated to the U.S. 50 or 60 years ago. Members of the group seem to have a fondness for plaids, sometimes speak with a brogue and have been known to use such other names as Williams, Stewart, McDonald, McMillan, Gregg and Johnstone. Their knowledge of the law and its loopholes has kept them operating with relative impunity.

These days there are telltale signs that the Williamsons have reached their traditional summering grounds, metropolitan New York and northern New Jersey. "Yes, they're here again," sighs Leo Powelstock, a Better Business Bureau executive in Paramus, N.J. "I personally toured four locations recently—including motels where they previously stayed—and I saw the small trucks parked next to expensive, late-model cars. It's the Williamsons, all right. I'm sure of that."

Mr. Powelstock should know. He has been following the Williamsons for years and knows their *modus operandi* well. He explains how the Williamson caravan pulls into a convenient motel and arranges for a telephone answering service and a mail drop. Then the group's trucks set forth to ply the trade.

Invariably the trucks contain large vats of a liquid (probably mostly oil) that the Williamsons bill as "weather sealer." The trucks pull up to a promising home, and the men ring the doorbell and launch into stories about how they've just finished up a "big job down the street" and have "a little bit of material left over." They offer the homeowner a "good deal," and all too often the homeowner takes it.

That's what happened to a Queens housewife in New York City. "These two men came around in a truck and said they'd do repair work for a very reasonable price," she says. "Well, the roof had been leaking. So I talked to Rosie, my neighbor, and we decided the men must be reliable since I'd seen their truck around the neighborhood before. Then I called my husband at work, and he said it was ok."

The men wanted $150, but the housewife talked them down to $125. The men asked for cash; the housewife offered them a check. The men replied that they would only accept a check if the housewife made it out to herself, accompanied them to the bank and cashed the check there. That didn't appeal to the housewife ("I don't drive around with strange men in trucks") so she went down the street to borrow the money.

"I was gone about 20 minutes," she says, "and when I got back, Rosie said to me, 'They're finished.' I said, 'They're finished? How can a job like this take only 20 minutes?' And one of the men said, 'Lady, are you looking for trouble?' He gave me a receipt with a guarantee and told me not to go upstairs to inspect because everything was still wet."

Eventually, of course, the rains came—and with them, the leaks and the almost inevitable phone call to the Better Business Bureau. The BBB told the housewife it sounded like the Williamsons.

Other homeowners report similar horror stories. One housewife paid $300 for a resurfacing job on her driveway, then watched as the resurfacing washed off in the first rain. Another told the BBB of a similar resurfacing job: The sticky material didn't dry for three months, and meanwhile people tracked it all over her house. A BBB bulletin tells of a $300 house-painting job that "defies description in terms of its shoddiness (and) sloppiness," its splattered paint, wrong colors and "missed portions throughout."

While the menfolk are out peddling painting and resurfacing jobs, the female Williamsons keep busy. "The women go from door to door selling cheap lace," says Mr. Sisapel of the BBB of Metropolitan New York.

"They give a sob story about having to sell their 'heirlooms from the old country' . . . but, of course, the material is virtually worthless."

The lace business aside, the Williamsons may rake in as much as $500 a day from a single truck, the BBB estimates. They have generally left an area by the time complaints to the BBB start flooding in, and arrests hold little terror for them in any case. That's because few of their activities can be defined as felonies. "When arrested, as they often are, gang members usually jump bail," says an inspector in New York's Department of Consumer Affairs. "They regard such disbursement as normal operating expenses."

—WILLIAM MATHEWSON

The Forest's Prime Evil

ARMED with flashlights, lances and lengths of chain, larcenous hunters are roaming the woods and waterways of the Pacific Northwest in search of a strange quarry—the untamed Douglas fir log.

The game is far from dangerous (no one can recall seeing a cornered log fight back), and the hunt is profitable. A prime log filched from field or stream may bring up to $125 today.

That's a lot more than it was worth not long ago, and the economics aren't lost on the folks in the area. More and more of them are taking to boat and pickup truck to snatch errant logs, cut them up for their own use, sell them to mills or even slip them into the black market for export. Log poaching, long a minor irritation to law enforcement officials, now is becoming a major headache. The reason is simple: Lumber prices are at record highs.

The poachers risk jail if caught. Under Oregon and Washington law, logs belong to the company whose brand they bear or, if they are unbranded, to the state. Poachers can be prosecuted either for a misdemeanor or for grand larceny.

State forestry personnel and private citizens licensed as special log patrolmen say thieves are zeroing in on the more valuable species, including cedar as well as Douglas fir. "Arrests for cedar log theft are more than double the usual rate," says John Griffiths, chief of law enforcement and log patrolling for the Washington State Department of Natural Resources.

Poachers recently pulled off what is believed to be the biggest log heist in history. A raft of more than 500 Douglas fir logs valued at over $17,000 disappeared one night from a busy storage area on the Willamette River a couple of miles from Portland.

Authorities figure the brigands used a tugboat to haul the logs alongside a waiting ship and then loaded them for export, all in about six hours. "You could have robbed Brink's a lot easier," laments Tony Smith, president of the towboat company that was storing the logs. "It's amazing—to me and to my insurance company." (Mr. Smith is being sued by the logs' owners).

Even with a tugboat, logs are hard to hide or handle. The average Douglas fir section is about 36 feet long and 18 inches thick. It weighs hundreds of pounds. "You can't get rid of them through your normal fence," allows Mr. Griffiths.

Consequently, most poachers like to get their logs cut up just as quickly as possible. Two were caught recently in Washington State where they were running a shuttle service between a cedar grove and a nearby shingle mill. Working with chain saws and a pickup truck, they cut enough cedar to make three round trips to the mill at about $100 a truckload before suspicious mill hands alerted authorities.

A few years ago, six enterprising poachers set up their own secret sawmill in a thick forest near Dead Man's Curve, 60 miles down the Columbia River from Portland. Tipped off by an alert area resident, the chief investigator of the Oregon State Forestry Department led a raid on the hidden mill. The raiders found it operating full tilt on a supply of more than 200 logs bearing the brands of 15 different companies. The mill was dismantled and the operators fined; the log owners declined to press grand larceny charges.

The forestry departments get considerable help in their enforcement efforts from the unsalaried citizen-patrolmen, numbering 17 in Oregon and 32 in Washington. In addition to spotting poachers, the patrolmen pick up stray unbranded logs, which are sold at auction by the state.

They get 60% of the sale price, a hefty incentive in these days of sky-high timber prices. Richard Wilson, a log patrolman who buzzes around Puget Sound in a 20-ton converted World War II landing craft, collected 300 stray logs in one recent month. His share of the take: $9,100.

The work can be hazardous, however. Enforcement officials say that in the rough and ready woodlands, a loose log is viewed as fair game no matter what the state statutes say. "The law doesn't sit too well in the woods," says Norris Joyce, Oregon's chief log investigator.

When log patrolman Wilson recently approached a beach to retrieve a big cedar log, a man appeared. Leveling a double-barreled shotgun at the patrolman, the man told him to "get the hell out of there." Mr. Wilson did just that.

—W. STEWART PINKERTON JR.

Modern-Day Rustlers

RUSTLERS are on the prowl again in the West. But instead of herding off cattle, these modern-day thieves are making off with an assortment of wild animals from zoos and concerns that provide trained animals for movies and television productions.

A baby tiger valued at $750 was stolen from the zoological gardens of the San Francisco Zoological Society one night. A $300 ape was stolen from the society's Children's Zoo. Two mountain lion cubs, valued about $1,000 and slated for appearance in two television series, were stolen from the game preserve of Africa, U.S.A., near Los Angeles.

Jungleland, another Los Angeles-area concern that supplies animals to Hollywood, lost two matched llamas, a trained sea lion, a trained European white fallow deer and an African pygmy goat during a six-week period. An official of the concern valued the five animals at more than $2,000.

Zoo officials and animal dealers say there's no indication that the unusual rash of California wild animal thefts is the result of an organized rustling operation. Keepers figure many animals are stolen by individuals stimulated at least in part by television shows depicting wild animals as sympathetic creatures who want them as pets, but at least one zoo official says stolen wild animals frequently wind up in small traveling road shows and in roadside animal displays aimed at pulling tourists off the freeways to buy trinkets.

A young San Francisco hippie was apprehended in the theft of the baby tiger and turned over to juvenile authorities after admitting he stole the animal. He and a companion (San Francisco police are still searching for him) stole the tiger cub, the youth said, because they wanted it for a pet but they ended up selling it to the Hermosa Reptile & Wild Animal Farm, Hermosa Beach, Calif., for $150 a few days later.

Ray Folson, owner of the farm, says the hippies told him they had obtained the baby tiger in Colorado and that his suspicions weren't aroused by the low price simply because baby tigers can be bought without much trouble in some parts of the country.

San Francisco's ape caper ended on a happier note. A. W. Kennard, animal keeper at the children's zoo, says the four-year-old ape had been gone about a week when it was spotted in the city's Golden Gate Park and returned. "I don't know how it was stolen," says Mr. Kennard. "But it was probably those darn hippies," he mutters.

In stealing the two baby mountain lions from Africa, U.S.A., rustlers also turned loose eight other animals, including "Clarence the cross-eyed lion," one of the concern's top television personalities. However, the eight animals were rounded up the next day and one of the baby mountain lions has since been recovered, according to an Africa, U.S.A., official. He won't comment on the recovery of the lion cub, except to say that it was found tied up at the front gate in the rain one recent morning. County sheriff's deputies are still trying to track down the second cub.

The theft forced producers of the Gentle Ben TV series to write the two mountain lion cubs out of the script and replace them with an anteater. Jungleland's owner is reluctant to discuss the thefts of the five animals from his 58-acre preserve. But law enforcement authorities say a former employe, currently in a state hospital, apparently spirited the animals away one or two at a time and sold them to a car dealer who peddles wild animals on the side. Jungleland still hasn't been able to get the animals back because the car dealer is said to have claimed he bought them in good faith from a man who was then a Jungleland employe.

Both Africa, U.S.A., and Jungleland have increased their security forces. Africa, U.S.A., has armed guards on duty 24 hours a day who have been specially trained to move among the 600 wild animals on its 22-acre preserve. A Jungleland official declines to describe its increased security in detail. "I'd just say I don't think anybody would want to prowl around here at night," he says.

Zoo officials in San Francisco, Los Angeles and San Diego say they haven't increased their security because of the rash of animal rustling, however. Aside from the thefts in San Francisco, they say most thefts involve pigeons, snakes, hawks and falcons apparently taken by youngsters. But a Los Angeles zoo official isn't so sure a youngster can be blamed for one theft there. "It was a domestic turkey," he recalls, "and it disappeared just before Christmas."

—BYRON CALAME

Trade Shows for Thieves

TRADE shows are an increasingly popular device for merchandisers to display their wares. They also are proving popular with thieves.

"It's a national epidemic," says Dolph Zapfel, managing director of the National Housewares Manufacturers Association. Some of the thievery is fairly dramatic; exhibitors still are talking about the $8,000 motorboat that was spirited from the National Boat Show at the New York Coliseum several years ago.

For the Coliseum, the Chicago International Amphitheatre and the other huge halls that cater to exhibitors, the problem has been getting worse. The National Housewares Exhibit in Chicago in July 1969 counted 724 crates, cartons or trucks of merchandise lost—more than in the 10 previous shows put together.

Visitors to one booth at that show were met by a hand-lettered sign that read, "Sorry, my samples have been stolen, but come in. I have pictures." Nathan H. Mager, who sponsors two large shows for antique dealers in New York City each year, says half a dozen exhibitors drop out each year due to thefts or the threat of thefts. Women dealers, he says, "get terribly emotional about it."

Nobody knows the total value of the losses. The crime flourishes despite expenditures on security ranging up to $50,000 per show. Blame focuses on larcenous workmen, show visitors, professional criminals, security guards and even the exhibitors themselves, some of whom allegedly sell items to one another, or swap them, and then report them stolen.

"More theft is created by carelessness than by any other source," says one businessman associated with trade shows. The $8,000 motorboat got stolen because its owner left the exit documents with the craft. The thief merely presented them and wheeled it past the guards.

Most of the thefts take place at night or during the chaotic period when a show is moving in or leaving. "At closing time a show looks like a hurricane hit," says one manager. "It's a shambles in four hours. People just want to get the hell out." The confusion provides opportunities for thievery.

The most prized items are consumer goods of high value and small size, like photographic equipment, and the suspects most often fingered by the exhibitors are the electricians, movers and other workmen who regularly work the shows. The International Ski & Winter Sports Show at the New York Coliseum offered many tempting wares. Harry Leonard, a promoter of the show, says that "we had to run around saying, 'Hey give that back!'" to workmen who brazenly helped themselves to clothing and audiovisual equipment used in the presentations.

"The workmen can watch for a time when there's a lull, or it's very crowded or there's a less heavily guarded show," says one trade show veteran. This man asserts he walked into a union hiring hall and spotted 12 office chairs that he had used in his exhibits. "I paid $11 each for them," he laments.

Rudolph Lang, president of Prestige Expositions Inc., a New York firm that arranges shows, orders his security people to "shake down" the Coliseum after every show in search of merchandise stashed away for later removal. So do other promoters. After one boat show, an outboard engine was found atop the heating system in the fourth floor ladies' room. Other items have been found buried in canvas laundry bins.

Daniel Sheridan, business agent for a Chicago local of the Machinery Movers, Riggers and Machinery Erectors Union, a source of labor for some trade shows, disputes the notion that workers steal from exhibits. "The natural fall guy is the workman," he says.

A big difficulty: Even when a thief is apprehended, exhibitors often decline to press charges. "I've had one prosecution in 30 years," says Mr. Lang, "so the thieves sort of thumb their noses at us."

Some exhibitors are too busy getting out of town to prosecute. Others apparently fear the consequences. "The workmen who steal manage to strike fear into every heart because they are retaliatory," says Mr. Leonard, the ski-show promoter. "If you prosecute, they will slow your show down. We are being threatened by a bunch of workers who think they have a license to steal."

One perhaps insoluble problem is that exhibition halls are large public buildings with many exits that can't be locked because of fire laws. McCormick Place, the new hall in Chicago, hopes to improve security by automation. A number of sensing points record movements of people and vehicles for a computer that pinpoints questionable occurrences—such as a fire door being opened when no fire alarm has been sounded.

—CAROL FALK

High-Risk Occupation

A NERVOUS-looking man steps out of an airplane, hurries along to catch up with passengers ahead and stays close to crowds in the terminal while waiting for his luggage. Outside, he passes up a line of taxicabs to wait in line for a limousine.

"Using taxis or cabs is quick death," he says. "It's too easy for a stickup man to knock you off when there aren't a lot of people around."

If the traveler sounds paranoid, he has a solid reason for it. In an inside vest pocket he carries $250,000 in diamonds. He is a diamond salesman, one of more than 400 who travel about the country or to Europe with as much as $1 million in precious stones. His trade has become a perilous one.

In the past few months, three diamond salesmen have been murdered. The most recent victim was Maurice R. Stamper, a salesman for Harry Winston Inc., the largest diamond wholesaler in the country. Mr. Stamper was found shot in the front seat of his 1968 Cadillac at Newark Airport. His attache case was missing, along with its contents, $436,000 in loose diamonds.

James B. White, head of the Jewelers' Security Alliance and a former FBI agent and Assistant U.S. Attorney, says diamonds are a prized target for underworld operatives because of their small size, high value and essentially untraceable nature. Only the man who has cut a stone can identify it, and then only when it weighs at least four carats, diamond experts say. Such a gem is as large as the tip of one's little finger.

Trade sources estimate that major stickups are running at the rate of five or six a year, with negligible recoveries of gems. The result: Increasing pressure from insurance companies for more stringent security precautions and increasing difficulty in hiring diamond salesmen, even though they make up to $80,000 a year.

And, predictably, some diamond salesmen are getting more cautious. One salesman talks to hardly anyone, not even policemen, when taking his wares around the country, and his New York home has been outfitted with a "pickproof" lock with magnetic tumblers. His wife is instructed to tell friends and callers that he is in the "optical supply business." His office has a bulletproof inner door. "You might say I lead a quiet, cautious life," he observes.

But police and insurance officials say few salesman are this careful. "There's a basic conflict between being a good salesman—outgoing and entertaining—and being a good security man," explains one Federal law enforcement official. Both police and insurance men cite indiscretions by salesmen who loudly proclaim their occupation in hotel lobbies or bars, or who take other chances, such as picking up women.

"This has got to be the loosest operation going," says the Federal lawman. Robert N. Gordon, president of Gordon Excess Coverage Ltd., a Lloyd's of London broker in New York City, believes that "most salesmen are completely unconcerned about security—they're a breed of people that just blabber."

"Many Lloyd's underwriters have already refused to write this type of coverage," Mr. Gordon says. "Others are prohibiting salesmen from carrying more than $125,000 or $250,000 worth of jewels and requiring that they use armored cars and security guards." Some salesmen known to be indiscreet are denied coverage altogether.

Jewelers and their insurers are considering a number of changes to tighten security. Salesmen's practices are under scrutiny, for instance. Harry Winston, president of the big New York firm, says that Mr. Stamper, the salesman murdered in Newark, had violated a cardinal rule by using his car to transport diamonds.

A major insurer points out the obvious temptation to robbers when salesmen are known to be carrying large quantities of gems. "Salesmen are crazy to carry more than $25,000 in gems at one time," he says. And he adds, "Anyone who takes his line into his hotel room is asking to be killed." This insurance company, like several others, refuses to insure salesmen going to Chicago —the city with the worst reputation for robberies—unless they are accompanied by an armed guard.

Use of guards is increasing, since even careful salesmen are prone to attacks. Jacques S. Hauser, a New York salesman, was assaulted in a crowded Tampa hotel. He was chased from the hotel and fatally shot in a bus depot a block away. Diamonds worth $100,000 were taken.

Many wholesale jewelers have arrived at an elementary solution to the problem—the U.S. mails. "We recommend that diamonds be mailed at all times," says one underwriter. This has precedent; Mr. Winston sent the $1 million Hope Diamond (44.5 carats) to the Smithsonian Institution by registered mail a few years ago.

But the mails present problems. The jewelry business, headquartered along Manhattan's 47th Street between 5th and 6th Avenues, is highly competitive, and using the mails involves a costly loss of time.

One man who should know—a diamond thief—confirms that the mails complicate his trade. "Once something goes into a post office," he says, "it's almost impossible to get it out." This thief, now on parole after being in jail for armed robbery, was interviewed through an arrangement with John J. McCarthy, associate director of the Bureau of Special Services, New York State Division of Parole.

The thief emphasizes that diamond robbers work with patience and care, often staking out a salesman's home to learn his habits and hiring assistants to check on airport arrivals. Killings may occur, he says, when the victim struggles, when he recognizes his assailant or when the attacker "just doesn't want any witnesses."

Information on trips planned by salesmen comes from Mafia informants in big jewelry firms and insurance companies, or from overhearing indiscreet gossip in the trade. And a chief market also is the Mafia. "Anyone stealing over $100,000 in stones has to do business with the mob," says the thief. "No one else has that much ready cash."

But the thief, who has to sell at a discount, gets only 33% to 40% of the gems' real value. The "fence" who arranges for their resale gets about 10%. Nevertheless, says this thief, "You don't need more than a few diamond hits a year" to prosper.

—Ronald Kessler

Gangsters Abroad

AMERICAN gangsters are preparing to move into London in a big way—and the move may well be merely the first step toward a major invasion of Europe by U.S. organized crime.

The Mafia and its several affiliates and subsidiaries in the United States, collectively known as the Syndicate, already are thought to have some interests in gambling operations scattered around the Continent. But investigators believe these are very minor investments, and there's little indication the Mob has thus far extended its own direct activities much beyond U.S. shores —except, of course, for the Mafia's strongholds in its native Sicily.

Now, however, there is persuasive evidence that the Syndicate is preparing for a big overseas push to England, where a burgeoning gambling industry offers a chance to gain an invaluable European foothold. Talks with government officials and with well-placed informants in London and in the U.S. reveal that the Mob already has quietly acquired interests in several London casinos and is working closely with other casinos to enhance the glamor and profitability of the British gambling industry by trying to lure big-time gamblers overseas.

These activities appear, moreover, to be simply preparation for an even bigger step: A wave of big investments that would put much of England's gambling activity firmly in the grip of the Syndicate, coupled with moves to bring England's entire collection of native, independently operated rackets under the control of the U.S. Mob. "American gangsters could wind up owning this town," says a U.S. Embassy official in London who is close to the situation.

Indeed, the rackets that could potentially wind up under Mafia control include the numbers game, protection shakedowns, smuggling and narcotics—activities that already exist in England but aren't now controlled by any central underworld power.

The Mob's expansion-mindedness stems in part, at least, from a feeling that its horizons in the U.S. are becoming a bit limited. The Syndicate's opportunities to control gambling have dwindled steadily as industrialists, led by billionaire Howard Hughes, have increasingly taken over Las Vegas casinos and ousted some—but by no means all—of the criminals there. Furthermore, concentrated efforts by law enforcement agencies in other states are making it increasingly difficult to set up gambling operations outside Nevada.

Even more important, a major Justice Department campaign against organized crime, launched by former Attorney General Robert Kennedy, has become increasingly effective in recent years in harassing Syndicate operations of all types in the U.S. A "strike force" plan whereby Federal authorities coordinate with local officials in selected cities is putting intense heat on the Mob. The Justice Department's list of arrested Mafia leaders has been growing steadily.

England, by contrast, offers several advantages for the Mob. The gambling industry is relatively new, dating back to the legalizing of gambling in private clubs in 1960, and it's growing rapidly. The monthly "handle," or volume, at one big London club, for example, jumped from about $360,000 in September 1967 to about $1.4 million in August of 1968. Moreover, the British government doesn't levy special taxes on gambling casino receipts, as Nevada does. It merely levies ordinary property and income taxes on the clubs and their owners.

Equally important is the Mob's confidence that it can simply get away with more in England, at least for a while, than it can in the U.S. British authorities have little experience with organized crime, and Syndicate leaders hope this will make them slow to react.

For the moment, the Syndicate is refraining from a wide-open push into London until it sees how England implements a new gaming law that requires for the first time that casinos be licensed. The law also sets up machinery for official control of gambling, which currently is only loosely regulated. It's not likely that the law will deter the Syndicate from moving in, but Mob leaders evidently see no reason to commit themselves fully until they see what form the regulation will take.

Their eagerness is evident, however, in one offer recently made to the owners of a major casino in London. A source associated with the casino says "Mafia representatives" offered to pay $1.5 million for a 30% interest in the casino if the present owners get a license under the new law. The offer is almost twice the current estimated market value of such an interest, and the source says the owners are "thinking hard about it."

The Syndicate's interest in England dates back to the 1960 betting and gaming act that legalized certain forms of gambling. Because a principal aim was to make it legal for churches to raise money through raffles and other games, the bill was dubbed the "vicars' emancipation."

The law had some unforeseen effects. Gambling casinos remained outlawed under the act, but private gaming clubs were made legal. Enterprising gamblers simply began opening casinos and calling them clubs, making customers "join" by paying a small fee at the door.

Before the British government quite realized what it had started, gambling clubs were feeding so much foreign currency, particularly dollars, into the country's stumbling economy that the thought of closing them down was out of the question. The number continued to grow until by late 1968 there were more than 1,000 in the country, about half in London. Their annual volume is an estimated $1.8 billion.

Another effect of the 1960 act was to make it legal for pubs and other establishments to install slot machines for the entertainment of their customers. A place could install only two machines, however, and they couldn't accept any coin larger than a six-pence piece.

The slot machines were the first result of the law to catch the attention of U.S. mobsters. The Syndicate wasn't interested in operating them, but it was interested in the market possibilities for machines. The Mob at that time had a number of slot machines going to rust in U.S. warehouses from casinos it had been forced to abandon in Havana after Fidel Castro took over the Cuban government.

So Antonio (Tony Ducks) Corallo, a captain in the New York Mafia family then headed by Thomas (Three-Finger Brown) Luchese, was dispatched to London to try to sell the machines. His connections were discovered, however, and it wasn't long before he was barred from England.

But Corallo did get into the country long enough to decide it had great potential for the Mob. He found that, although a number of criminal gangs operated in England, they didn't have the financing or the experience to organize their rackets into a powerful national network.

Unable to return to England himself, Corallo sent an emissary to make contact with the British gangsters and try to arrange an alliance with American underworld forces. Corallo's immediate goal was a numbers network in England similar to those operating in major U.S. cities.

Corallo made one mistake, however. He chose as his emissary an informer for the Federal Bureau of Investigation. The man, New York attorney Herbert Itkin, was responsible several years later for uncovering the kickback scheme involving Corallo and James L. Marcus, a key aide to New York Mayor John V. Lindsay.

On his trips to England for Corallo, Mr. Itkin made full reports of his activities to American officials in London. He limited his criminal contacts to underworld has-beens, not the real crime leaders in the country, and Corallo's numbers empire never came to be.

As gambling clubs began to multiply in London, however, Syndicate leaders began to send other representatives to see how best to take advantage of the situation. About this time, Dino Cellini arrived in London. He had for many years been a trusted lieutenant of Meyer Lansky, one of the overlords of organized crime in the United States and a builder of gambling empires in Las Vegas, Florida, Cuba and the Bahamas.

In England, Cellini started a school for croupiers and then became an "adviser" to the Colony Sporting Club, one of the posh casinos in London's West End. Eventually he rose to the job of manager and became a director of the club.

Cellini brought actor George Raft to England, and

the club was rechristened George Raft's Colony Sporting Club. An old friend of Meyer Lansky and his late partner, Bugsy Siegel, Mr. Raft was working at El Casino de Capri, a gambling house in Havana controlled by Lansky, just before Castro took over Cuba.

After studying the backgrounds of the Messrs. Raft and Cellini, the British Home Office barred the two men from England. Cellini hasn't entirely severed his relationship with the Colony, however. He still organizes groups of gamblers and sends them on junkets to the club.

The Home Office has also barred Lansky from England, but U.S. investigators say they are convinced he currently controls one or more major casinos in London through a front organization and is trying to buy into several others. Lansky has worked with Mafia leaders throughout his adult life, and several high-ranking Mafia men are believed to be sharing the profits of clubs he controls in London.

Other Mafia figures are working hard to carve their own empires in England. A group led by Angelo Bruno, leader of the Cosa Nostra in Philadelphia and a member of its national ruling council, flew to England in 1966. According to Scotland Yard officials, his group not only visited every major club in London but also stopped at big casinos in such other British cities as Birmingham, Manchester and Liverpool.

The purpose of the tour, investigators say, was to determine how Mafia families not yet involved in England might take advantage of the gambling boom. The gangsters concluded there was plenty of money to be made not only by trying to get interests in the clubs but also by providing services to clubs not controlled by them.

When they returned to the U.S., they began providing other services, which included organizing junkets to selected clubs in England, supplying credit information on American gamblers to casinos and collecting debts owed to clubs by Americans. Angelo Bruno went into the junket business himself through fronts, as did Pinky Panarelli, Cosa Nostra chief in central Massachusetts, and some other men with known Mafia ties.

The British government frowns on such junkets, in which gamblers are flown in at special rates on a group basis, but it tolerates them because of the dollars they bring in. Besides its genuine customers, the Mafia also sometimes sends "mechanics," or crooked gamblers, to try to clean out casinos that don't buy its services.

Once the new gaming law is fully in effect, U.S. authorities believe, the Mafia will try to buy the casinos it now serves. For the moment, though, it must keep its links with the casinos as tenuous as possible. A gaming board, created under the new law, soon will be examining the ownership, finances and policies of casinos preparatory to licensing them. Sir Stanley Raymond, chairman of the gaming board, warns that licenses will go only to casinos run by persons of the "highest repute."

To the Mob, however, Sir Stanley's warning simply means that it can't move in until the licenses have been issued. Then, presumably, it will see what sort of arrangements it can make with the reputable individuals and groups that hold the licenses.

The law also gives the home secretary power to make regulations to correct abuses as they arise. Sir Stanley says the combination of licensing and regulations may well reduce the number of clubs in London to 200 or 300 from the present 1,000 or so. Some operators, he says, may decide that the "proposition is not so attractive when they know the conditions that will be laid down."

Critics of the law have expressed doubt, however, that the board will have either the manpower or the budget to supervise casinos adequately. One former member of Parliament contends the law is "a gift to the racketeers."

One factor that's particularly encouraging to Mafia leaders is a misconception apparently held by some British officials that practically all U.S. gangsters are of Italian descent. Meyer Lansky, easily one of the most powerful gangsters in the world, visited Britain a few years ago, and authorities didn't realize he had been there until he was gone. But a short time later, a group of men—all swarthy and bearing Italian names—arrived at London Airport and were immediately surrounded by immigration officials, who held them for several hours until they discovered that the men were carpenters on their way to work on the U.S. Embassy.

British officials are not always so naive, however. In 1966 the Mob sent a man to London to develop links with local gangsters. He sought out leaders of one of the most powerful gangs in England, men so imaginative they are said to have once contemplated kidnapping the Pope. The Mafia evidently intended to use the gang as the nucleus of an organization that would eventually direct all rackets in Great Britain.

What the gang needed most for such an organization was money, and the Mafia representative showed its leaders how they could make a lot of money quickly by handling stolen securities from Canada and the United States. The group even set up its own bank to receive the securities, stamp them to make them look legitimate, then send them to agents in Europe who allegedly used them as collateral for big loans.

As evidence of these arrangements, British authorities found in the London hotel room of the Mafia's agent $90,000 worth of negotiable bonds stolen from an eminent New York law firm, and police searching his New York City apartment discovered a code book allegedly used in sending cables to the English gang and its European associates.

"This demonstrates just how far organized crime forces are willing to go to get firmly established in England," says a U.S. official who has followed the Mob's international operations for years. "They've had some setbacks, but they're going to keep trying. There is a lot of money to be made over there, and they're not going to pass it up."

—NICHOLAS GAGE

The Big Payoff

WILLIAM Barnett was looking for an apartment a few years ago but he just couldn't find one to suit him. And then the "perfect solution" struck him: The young New Yorker typed a card identifying himself as a "city housing inspector." No sane landlord, he reasoned, would turn down a building inspector's request for an apartment.

He picked the building he wanted, met the landlord and flashed his card. But before he could say a word about wanting an apartment, the landlord handed him $50 in cash.

The startled and delighted Barnett quickly began a new career. Equipped with only the crudely made card, he visited 200 landlords and extorted from them more than $10,000 in four months. Not a single landlord complained to the city. Barnett was caught only after one owner complained of a subsidiary business the "inspector" had started: Making landlords cash bad checks.

Barnett was convicted and jailed, which was bad luck for him. For if he were still making his rounds his take would surely be bigger than ever. Bribes, both big and small, have become as familiar to New Yorkers as are the crowds on the subways. Nobody knows how many millions of dollars are slipped under the table in New York every year, but many residents think the problem has reached epidemic proportions. They say bribes commonly procure anything from choice apartments to extra garbage collections to state inspection stickers for cars that could barely meet the standards of a high-class junkyard.

Payoffs affect life everywhere, of course. But New York's problem is generally thought to be among the nation's worst. Though thousands of New Yorkers sternly resist making any payoffs, many say it is getting hard to live in the city without offering endless bribes of various sorts. The problem is especially rough if one is in business, they say.

Take the Manhattan business consultant who recently moved his office from a Midtown office building to an East Side apartment house. A few days before moving day, an installer from New York Telephone Co. called. "The installer asked me to come down to the new place right away," the consultant recalls. "I asked him why, because there were signs indicating where I wanted the new phones. He said he had to put in a big black box and he wanted my advice because it might ruin the decor," the consultant says.

"So I went to the apartment, and he said, 'Gee I can't get to it today. How about a couple of weeks?' So I gave him $10, and he installed the phones immediately."

That was just the start. The consultant packed four large cartons and started to move them to the new office one night. But the night custodian in the office building refused to unlock the large nonrevolving doors to let the cartons out. "I had to give him $5," the consultant sighs. "Then about an hour later his supervisor came and hit the ceiling" over opening the locked doors "so it cost me another five bucks."

Then came the new place. The superintendent

asked for a $20 "gratuity" before the move. But when the consultant needed two minor repairs, he had to give the "super" $25 to make them. "Even after I gave him the money, it took him three days to get here," the consultant laments.

Payoffs are an especially hot issue these days because of widespread reports of massive police corruption. Patrick V. Murphy, the city's new police commissioner, recently said he planned to increase the staff that investigates police corruption charges and handles discipline.

Mr. Murphy conceded there was "no question" that there had been recent examples of police corruption. He said officers were subject "to tremendous pressures and temptations" and that he would encourage businessmen and citizens to avoid giving patrolmen free food, services and other gifts.

William H. T. Smith, first deputy police commissioner, has urged policemen to arrest people who offer bribes. He contends this would be the most effective way to discourage the public from trying to corrupt the police. And the Police Academy should increase emphasis and training in resisting corruption and making arrests for bribery, he says.

Corruption in the police goes far beyond snitching apples from fruit stands. For instance, three police officers recently arrested were found with a list of 50 restaurants and other businesses in their West Side Manhattan precinct. A dollar figure—presumably the amount of a regular payoff—followed each name.

Many New Yorkers don't fully accept the city's payoff reputation, however. "New York is rampant in low-and-middle-level corruption, but it's surprisingly uncorrupt at a high level," says Amitai Etzioni, chairman of Columbia University's sociology department. He contends that if influence peddling to wealthy businessmen and the corruption of high local officials are included, many small towns "are a hell of a lot more corrupt than New York."

Yet most New Yorkers agree that such factors as the huge city bureaucracy, the miles of red tape that needs cutting, the housing shortage and the "tradition" of graft all make the city ripe for corruption. "The city (government) is one of the most complex and stale bureaucracies there is," Prof. Etzioni says. "Corruption is one way of making a social system work. In effect you're paying for services rendered."

Robert K. Ruskin, the city's investigation commissioner, disagrees. "If you're getting a special service, someone else is being ignored who perhaps can't afford to pay."

One problem investigators have is that New Yorkers are so willing to pay bribes without complaining. There are many reasons for this. There is often only a thin line between a payoff and a genuine tip, and some bribe-givers honestly believe they are merely tipping. Altruism also plays a role. A real estate executive, who says he constantly makes payoffs, explains: "Maybe it's because people get paid so little. Payoffs are not only accepted, they're depended upon in order to maintain a certain standard of living." Others contend it is simpler to shell out the money than to argue and complain. Still others simply like to "buy" people.

But many New Yorkers feel they have little choice in numerous circumstances. Persons involved in construction or ownership of buildings seem particularly vulnerable. The hapless owner of an Upper West Side restaurant recalls his woes building a new addition recently:

"When the walls are all up, the big-shot inspector

finally comes in. 'Is that all fire-proof?' he wants to know. I show him all the documents, and he says, 'That doesn't mean anything; I've got to see it. I'd have to tear all the walls down. So I tell him 'Come in the back room and you can see it there.' I gave him fifty bucks and everything was settled."

A contractor soon afterwards presented a $439 bill to the restaurateur for electrical wiring. The bill included an unspecified payoff to get the wiring approved, the contractor claimed.

But even paying bribes didn't eliminate trouble. "The inspector okays the wiring without seeing the job, so I have no way of knowing whether it's defective," moans the restaurateur. "My overhead bulbs are burning out every other day, and they cost $2.75 apiece. But when I complain to the electrician, he tells me the inspector approved the job."

Many city building inspectors have a nonnegotiable, uniform, city-wide scale of payoffs, some architects and construction executives say. Approvals typically cost $50 for a brownstone alteration, $100 for a house and $200 for a small industrial facility, they say. Inspectors have reportedly raised the payoff scale in recent years to parallel the inflation in other construction costs.

Apartment dwellers also must often pay bribes— and sometimes in bizarre forms. A young, long-haired couple recently wanted to sublet a West Side Manhattan apartment from an artist. The artist talked of demanding $500, then settled for an unusual price: One pound of hashish.

"It was a good deal," says the husband. "The stuff cost us $45 in North Africa, and he could get $1,200 for it by selling it in ounces. So we both came out ahead."

Payoffs to obtain rent-controlled apartments with

unusually low rents have been common. But in the current tight apartment market, a person must often pay key money even for a high-rent apartment. One young woman was able to move into an apartment in the elegant East 70s only after she agreed to the superintendent's demand for a $50 "tip" each Christmas.

In their effort to crack down on the wave of bribery, Mayor John Lindsay and other officials are running into some unusual opposition: The bribe payers are complaining. An example: An architect who traditionally has walked into the city's buildings department each Christmas with a case of liquor complains of his most recent visit. "Somebody ran over to me, turned me around and paraded me out. So I had to deliver every single bottle surreptitiously at night to people's homes."

—STANFORD N. SESSER

Curbing Fraud

THE complaining letter came from an inmate in a New Jersey prison. "It's a shame that these con experts can get away with their chicanery," the prisoner wrote. A New York City bookstore, it seems, had ignored his mail order for some books but kept the money that came with it.

To the rescue came New York City's Department of Consumer Affairs, a fledgling agency that pursues shady or delinquent merchants on behalf of all sorts of consumers. Department investigators called at the bookstore and secured a refund for the inmate.

There was some skepticism when Bess Myerson Grant, a former Miss America (1945) and television personality, was designated the city's first commissioner of consumer affairs by Mayor John V. Lindsay in February of 1969. Many figured that the attractive, 45-year-old brunette would content herself with a glamorous sideshow for consumers.

Apparently they were wrong. Miss Myerson is taking her job seriously, and the city administration is backing the effort. Her hamburger raiders, for instance, have become notorious among restaurant proprietors. In the last half of 1969, more than 500 eateries were raided, and 185 summonses were handed out for patties that weren't all beef. Violations mean a $100 fine.

The consumer protection program is a comprehensive one. In November of 1969 the city put into effect a truth-in-pricing law that requires merchants to label most food products on a per-unit basis such as "10 cents a pound," no matter what the size of the container. In addition, a consumer protection act considered to be one of the toughest such statutes in the nation has been signed into law by Mr. Lindsay.

The consumer protection act is designed to end a host of abuses. For instance, it gives the city the power to sue an unscrupulous merchant on behalf of all consumers cheated by the firm. Individuals usually lack the resources to undertake suits.

Mrs. Grant also has ventured to take tough stands on issues dear to consumers. She lashed out at Blue Cross hospital insurance rates and tried—unsuccessfully—to block a 43% rate hike in the city. She has urged customers of troubled New York Telephone Co. not to pay their bills if the service isn't good, and she has even taken on the Good Housekeeping seal, charging that it is "a fraud on the public"—a charge the magazine vehemently denies.

Consumer experts elsewhere seem impressed by Mrs. Grant's performance so far. "Bess is highly effective, a real solid consumer advocate," says Virginia Knauer, President Nixon's special assistant for consumer affairs. Ralph Nader, the dean of consumer advocates, says, "New York could literally become the model for all other cities to follow."

That may be happening already. Mrs. Grant's department has received requests for information on its programs from more than 40 city and state agencies around the nation. City officials from Baltimore and Jacksonville, Fla., spent time in New York recently picking up pointers on consumer protection.

Predictably, Mrs. Grant also has ruffled some feathers, "She gets a little flamboyant in her PR tactics," says Ralph Gross, president of New York's Commerce and Industry Association. Mr. Gross was particularly irked by Mrs. Grant's testimony about the telephone company before the state Public Service Commission. "She flatly said they didn't deserve a rate increase before all the facts were in," he complains. "It was clearly an area where she had no authority."

Others complain that Mrs. Grant, the wife of a prominent Manhattan attorney, had little previous administrative experience and little previous identification with consumerism, other than appearing on television shows sponsored by makers of toothpaste and soap flakes. Mrs. Grant, who originally wanted to be a concert pianist, concedes that she was surprised when Mayor Lindsay offered her the job.

"I thought it was a great opportunity to put myself on the line to see if I could really deliver," she says.

The returns aren't in yet, but nobody is accusing Mrs. Grant of not trying. "Our cup runneth over," says John Hopkins, executive vice president of the New York Retail Merchants Association. "It's difficult to keep up with what they're preparing for us next." Mr. Hopkins recently jousted with Mrs. Grant over the truth-in-pricing regulations.

Associates say Mrs. Grant does her homework and takes an active role in formulating new programs, besides serving as the city's official consumer spokesman at various public hearings in New York and in Washington. She is assisted by Henry Stern, a 34-year-old lawyer and a former assistant city administrator who oversees the department's operations, and Simon Lazarus, another young lawyer who handles legal questions.

To critics of her publicity techniques, Mrs. Grant

says it is vital to educate consumers and to make New Yorkers aware that the department exists. "One of our greatest weapons," she says, "is to publicize that a particular industry has been flagrantly abusive. And if we can show there is going to be punishment, it's a great deterrent."

However, other city officials occasionally wince at the latest revelation by Mrs. Grant's department. A recent press release reported on a "nut by nut" study of several brands of mixed nuts. The survey's conclusion: "Each can had a positive plethora of peanuts and a frustrating dearth of all the other delicious-but-more-expensive goodies."

Getting the public's attention was a problem at first. Consumer protection activities had been spread among several city agencies. The Department of Consumer Affairs was created in October 1968 by merging the old departments of markets and licensing. It was given the task of developing a program of consumer protection and education.

To drum up business, the department has decreed that each of the some 30,000 establishments it now licenses in 110 types of businesses (parking lots, used car dealers and employment agencies are among them) must prominently display a sign bearing the department's 24-hour-a-day telephone number for complaints. Consumers are urged to register their gripes in person. And a "consumobile" roams the city taking complaints.

The department recently issued a handbook entitled "How to Sue Someone in New York Small Claims Court." The pamphlet provides instructions on how to fill out subpoena forms, maps showing the locations of the courts and information on how to get money from a defendant who loses in court but refuses to pay: "Your next step is to go to either the sheriff or a marshal. A list of their addresses is in appendix B at the end of this book."

Such tactics seem to be working. About 2,300 complaints now are received each month, more than double the rate of March 1969, when Mrs. Grant took office. The response leads many officials to believe that the most effective place for a consumer protection agency is at the city level rather than the state or Federal level.

"We're closer to the people," says Mrs. Grant. "It dilutes some of the cynicism and some of the hopelessness."

Until recently, however, the department's powers have been limited. It has had the power to revoke licenses, and it has undertaken to enforce old city regulations that had been largely ignored. This was the case with the hamburger inspections.

In some cases, the department beefed up regulations in areas where it already had authority. In August 1969, it drew up new rules for parking lot owners. They now must carry a minimum of $100,000 in personal injury liability insurance and are forbidden to move cars except when necessary to make space for newly arrived vehicles. They aren't allowed any longer to save reserve space for favored customers. It's considered doubtful that garages are uniformly heeding the latter two rules.

One of the department's most useful tools often has been moral suasion. A young New York City couple, for instance, recently discovered that time payments on a freezer they had contracted to buy ($27.50 a month for 36 months) totaled more than twice the usual retail cash price. Food purchases in the contract brought the payments to $92 a month. It was all in the fine print of the contract and technically legal, but department inspectors explained to the freezer company that the couple simply couldn't meet the payments and persuaded it to abrogate the contract. The couple also had large mortgage payments.

Some people with complaints haven't obtained satisfaction, however. A teacher recently wrote to say that she had been gypped by a travel agency that sold a package tour in Spain including hotel accommodations, limousine service and meals. The teacher and some friends who also signed up arrived to find no limousine, booked-up hotels and other inconveniences that cost her an extra $100 a week.

"It was a sad case, but there just wasn't much we could do," laments Ray Fitzgerald, who is in charge of complaints for the department. "We just didn't have any authority."

That has changed with the new consumer protection act. It gives the city authority to move against almost every type of shady practice, city officials say. The act specifically bans deceptive or unconscionable practices in the sale, lease, rental or loan of any consumer goods or services, or in the extension of consumer credit or in debt collecting.

Under the act's enforcement provisions, the department may obtain a court injunction against the illegal act. If a substantial number of people have been fleeced, the department may sue the merchant and obtain mass restitution so all the aggrieved customers can get their money back. The department isn't given authority to mete out punishments on its own, however.

Many states and cities, of course, already have laws dealing with consumer deception. And consumer agencies in Arizona, Delaware, Illinois, Iowa, Kansas, Missouri, New Jersey and North Dakota have power to get restitution for many consumers.

Philip Schrag, a lawyer who is chairman of the department's consumer advisory council, says that the

New York act will combine "all the best features" of other antifraud laws. Moreover, he says, the department plans to add eight lawyers to its current staff of six, to handle enforcement matters.

Mrs. Grant's most controversial foray has been the Good Housekeeping seal venture. Testifying before the National Commission on Product Safety in September 1969, she charged that the seal was misleading. She cited a department study that found 29% of consumers believing that the seal guaranteed adherence to Federal safety and quality standards. This isn't the fact.

Mrs. Grant said Good Housekeeping should make its standards available to the public and accept liability for personal and product injuries stemming from defects in the products it endorses. Good Housekeeping countercharged that Mrs. Grant's conclusions were "false and misleading" and said it applied "known criteria" in testing.

"We can't conceivably say to the consumer that the product she receives is a good one," says Ray Peterson, publisher of the magazine. "We say it *should* be a good one, after making tests of representative samples." The seal promises that Good Housekeeping will replace a defective product that it has endorsed or refund the buyer's money.

But Mrs. Grant's testimony may yet prove prophetic. In 1967 a California woman sustained a serious knee injury after slipping on a vinyl floor. She was wearing shoes that had the Good Housekeeping seal. A state appeals court in San Diego has ruled that the woman can sue Good Housekeeping for damages.

—W. STEWART PINKERTON JR.

Unlikely Crusader

A HOLLYWOOD casting director trying to fill the part of a relentless prosecuting attorney wouldn't give Robert M. Morgenthau a second look.

Mr. Morgenthau is a shy, polite lawyer who shuns the spotlight. He prefers the painstaking search for evidence of white-collar crime to the flamboyant pursuit of a bank robber. He never personally tries a case in court, preferring to stay in the background as an administrator.

Yet in his seven years as U.S. Attorney for the Southern District of New York, Mr. Morgenthau has been in the headlines as often as not. At the age of 49, he is firmly established as one of the nation's top prosecutors, even though he has concentrated on the complex fraud and securities cases that have been the despair of many of his colleagues and predecessors.

Indeed, it has been charged that Mr. Morgenthau is *too* relentless. Roy M. Cohn, the lawyer and businessman against whom Mr. Morgenthau in late 1968 obtained a 10-count indictment for mail and wire frauds, conspiracy and violation of securities rules, angrily retorted by charging that the prosecutor was carrying on a "vendetta" against him. Mr. Morgenthau is a liberal Democrat, and Mr. Cohn was chief legal aide to the late Sen. Joseph McCarthy in his Communist-hunting activities in the 1950s. In 1964, Mr. Cohn was acquitted of perjury and obstruction of justice charges growing out of another securities case brought by Mr. Morgenthau. That time around, Mr. Cohn also raised the "vendetta" charges.

Mr. Morgenthau won't comment on Mr. Cohn's allegations. "He (Mr. Cohn) was indicted by a Federal grand jury . . . and his guilt or innocence will be decided by a trial jury," he says.

The prosecutor's friends maintain that he is equally dogged in pursuing persons whose political philosophy is closer to his own. They cite the fact that in 1963 he obtained a conviction for tax evasion against James M. Landis, a former Harvard Law School dean who held top posts in the Roosevelt and Truman Administrations. Mr. Landis received a 30-day jail sentence.

It's clear that Mr. Morgenthau doesn't shy from initiating actions against well-known people, including some with political connections. Among those he has successfully prosecuted are millionaire industrialist Louis Wolfson, James L. Marcus, a former New York City water commissioner, and Johnny (Johnny Dio) Dioguardi, an alleged top Mafia figure.

Mr. Morgenthau's batting average isn't perfect, by any means. In addition to his failure to obtain a conviction of Mr. Cohn in 1964, he struck out in another highly sensitive case—the tax evasion trial of J. Truman Bidwell, who was chairman of the board of governors of the New York Stock Exchange when he was indicted.

It's widely agreed that Mr. Morgenthau's most notable contributions have stemmed from the nature of the cases he has tackled. He has scrutinized stock market manipulations to an extent believed to be unprecedented for his office, and he has focused what many law enforcement officials say is long overdue attention on broader aspects of white-collar crime.

"More than anyone, he has brought about an awareness of the great importance of diligent enforcement in this very complicated area," says Ramsey Clark. "Men who seek to be measured by statistics would never take these cases on. Any one of them counts for 100 or more ordinary prosecutions in terms of the investment of investigatory and prosecutory manpower."

Mr. Morgenthau's vigor in policing the securities industry has led to considerable interest in whom President Nixon will pick to succeed him in the $28,750-a-year post. Mr. Nixon touched off a campaign controversy with a pledge to give the securities industry a looser rein, and his U.S. Attorney appointment for the post Mr. Morgenthau now holds is expected to be a tipoff as to his approach to stock market regulation.

Mr. Morgenthau comes from a prominent and influential New York family. His father, Henry Morgenthau Jr., was Secretary of the Treasury under President Franklin D. Roosevelt, and his grandfather, Henry Morgenthau Sr., was U.S. ambassador to Turkey in the Administration of Woodrow Wilson.

Mr. Morgenthau was graduated from Amherst College and received his law degree from Yale Law School. From his law school graduation in 1948 until President Kennedy appointed him U.S. Attorney in 1961, he was with the New York law firm of Patterson, Belknap & Webb, which has a sizable corporate practice.

In 1962, he was persuaded to run for governor of New York on the Democratic ticket against the incumbent, Nelson Rockefeller. His campaign, generally judged to be one of the quietest and least effective in

New York political history, fell more than 500,000 votes short of victory.

The prosecutor acknowledges that he has many acquaintances in New York's financial and political communities and that this can prove awkward at times. "You go to a dinner, and sitting next to you is some important politician who is a friend of the man you are putting in prison," he says.

Fellow lawyers assert, however, that Mr. Morgenthau isn't at all receptive to appeals of friendship in cases his office handles. "If I asked him to look into a case as a favor to me, an old friend, it would be enough for him to pull out all stops trying to indict my client," a lawyer who is in private practice says only partly in jest.

Mr. Morgenthau doesn't run a one-man show by any means. His New York district contains more corporate headquarters, brokerage firms and banks than any other, and it's also the home of some top members of the Mafia, so it rates the largest staff of any U.S. Attorney. Indeed, his highly regarded staff of 73 Assistant U.S. Attorneys constitute about 10% of the U.S. total.

Mr. Morgenthau's office is "primus inter pares"—first among equals—of the 93 U.S. judicial districts, says Steve Sachs, U.S. Attorney for Maryland. "He runs a little Department of Justice," Mr. Sachs says.

From the start, Mr. Morgenthau decided to deploy a sizable segment of his forces to keep close tabs on white-collar offenses. The move reflected his belief that "it was important to show that the businessman or public official had no more immunity before the law than the little guy."

He created a five-man Securities Fraud Unit in his office, and he assigned 18 more assistants to it on a part-time basis. This unit departed from past practice by initiating major cases in the securities field instead of waiting for the Securities and Exchange Commission to commence such actions. At the same time, his assistants have worked closely with SEC investigators in the preparation of many cases.

Prosecuting business crime is a more difficult proposition than going after a hijacker or bank robber, Mr. Morgenthau asserts. "When someone robs a bank, everyone at least knows that a crime has been committed," he points out, "When someone commits a tax fraud, it may be years before anyone even knows that something wrong has been done."

In addition, businessmen who are brought to trial often can afford batteries of top lawyers, fully equipped to employ every legal maneuver to keep their clients free. Thus, litigation becomes involved and lengthy.

Mr. Morgenthau illustrates the time-consuming nature of prosecuting persons accused of white-collar crimes by citing a case his office brought against a New York accountant charged with bribing an Internal Revenue Service agent on behalf of a client.

He says that 10 agents of the Federal Bureau of Investigation and two Assistant U.S. Attorneys worked on the case for about six months before an indictment was obtained in 1961. "Then we had two guys preparing for the trial," he says. The accountant was convicted in 1963. He appealed the decision on technical grounds and won. He was retried and convicted again in 1966. The conviction was upheld by the U.S. Court of Appeals in 1967, and the Supreme Court later refused to review the case. The accountant then asked for a reduction of sentence, which was denied. An appeal from that decision recently was refused.

Mr. Morgenthau says that each appeal of the case tied up two of his assistants for several months. He adds that drawn-out cases of this sort aren't uncommon in his office.

According to Roy Cohn, Mr. Morgenthau's investigatory methods amount to harassment. Mr. Cohn has charged the prosecutor with making a "mockery" of the Federal grand jury system by using his subpoena power to "oppress, intimidate and harass" himself and his associates in obtaining the latest indictments, which stem from Mr. Cohn's involvement in the affairs of Fifth Avenue Coach Lines Inc., a New York firm. Mr. Cohn estimates that Mr. Morgenthau's office interrogated 700 persons, issued more than 1,000 subpoenas and spent more than $1 million in its investigation of him.

Mr. Morgenthau won't discuss the Cohn case, but he says he believes that "every safeguard" is given to the rights of defendants in Federal court actions and that those rights also extend to grand jury investigations. "If we public prosecutors improperly use the subpoena power, a defendant can move to set aside the subpoena. I could be censured by a court if I used it improperly," he says.

Some of Mr. Morgenthau's most celebrated legal victories have come in the securities law field. For example, Louis Wolfson's convictions were for obstructing an SEC probe into Merritt-Chapman & Scott Corp., which he controlled, and for his illegal sale of unregistered shares of another firm, Continental Enterprises Inc.

The prosecutor is investigating a broad securities case involving the alleged manipulation of the prices of several stocks traded on the American Stock Exchange, including Pentron Electronics Corp. and Terminal-Hudson Electronics Inc. This probe, which began some years ago, already has produced indictments against 43 persons.

Mr. Morgenthau's delving into business crime also has borne fruit in other areas. Johnny Dioguardi, for instance, was convicted of bankruptcy fraud. Obtaining the conviction required his prosecutors to possess considerable financial acumen, legal observers say.

Mr. Morgenthau's staffers, along with the FBI, are given much of the credit for untangling the financial transactions that led to the conviction of James L. Marcus, a friend and confidant of New York Mayor John Lindsay, for accepting a kickback as water commissioner from Anthony (Tony Ducks) Corallo, whom Federal investigators describe as a Mafia leader.

A prosecutor faces a substantial loss of prestige if he loses a case against a highly placed figure in business or politics, and Mr. Morgenthau successfully ran this risk in his prosecution of Marcus. "If the evidence against Marcus didn't hold up, Bob stood to be accused of making a political indictment" against New York's Republican city administration, says a former aide of Mr. Morgenthau.

Under Mr. Morgenthau, the New York U.S. Attorney's office has broken new ground in the prosecution of financial violations. In 1968 the prosecutor provoked the outrage of the nation's accounting profession by obtaining criminal convictions against two partners and an executive of the highly respected accounting firm of Lybrand, Ross Bros. & Montgomery. They were charged with conspiracy and fraud in concealing the fact that the head of Continental Vending Machine Corp. siphoned off over $3 million in company funds through an affiliate. Lybrand-Ross was Continental Vending's auditor.

Many accountants believed that Lybrand-Ross shouldn't be held responsible for the false statements of Continental Vending's officer, and Mr. Morgenthau says that numerous top accountants refused his requests to testify as expert witnesses for the Government in the matter. Many accountants still argue that the court's guilty verdict against the firm unfairly extends an auditor's responsibilities. The Lybrand-Ross defendants are appealing the convictions, for which they were fined but not jailed.

A former Assistant U.S. Attorney upholds Mr. Morgenthau's prosecution of the case. "Here's a case in which the defendants didn't steal and didn't get paid under the table, but Bob felt that the criminal laws had to be applied in a situation in which accountants disregarded the public interest," he says.

Mr. Morgenthau is attempting to further extend the scope of business law prosecutions with an investigation of the use of Swiss banks by American businessmen who want to evade U.S. taxes. Other U.S. Attorneys have had little success in breaking the tight secrecy that surrounds Swiss bank accounts. The probe, of course, won't necessarily produce any indictments.

—STANLEY PENN

On the Waterfront

ROSS Trucking Co. has a good thing going: A guarantee that about half the bananas imported into the New York area must be hauled from the docks in Ross trucks.

Three of the four major U.S. banana importers see to it that no competitor muscles in. The importers say Ross gets the work because the company is fast, efficient and reliable. Others, including a representative of the Waterfront Commission of New York Harbor, suspect it's because a key Ross employe is well-connected to the Mafia.

Law enforcement agencies are concerned about the proliferation of Mafia-owned and Mafia-controlled businesses, resulting from the reinvestment of the vast profits of organized crime. But Ross, with its employe who has been tied to the Mafia, raises a related question: Does the mere suggestion of a Mafia link give a firm a competitive advantage?

There isn't any evidence that Ross used illegal tactics to get its exclusive position at Port Newark, N.J., and Pier 13 on New York's East River. The three banana importers unload at these docks, and they won't sell their bananas (which include such brand names as Bonita and Cabana) to jobbers unless Ross gets the delivery work. The jobbers pay Ross' entire bill.

Jobbers are middlemen who buy green bananas from the importers and sell to retailers after the bananas ripen. The 23 trucks Ross operates haul bananas to jobbers within a 50-mile radius of New York City. (Ross' monopoly at the two piers doesn't apply to bananas going to more distant points.) Ross deals with 25 or more jobbers, it is estimated.

Some jobbers who use Ross get nervous when the name is mentioned. "Leave me out," says one. "This is strictly a cement-overcoat situation." Another says, "Look, I don't question the system." A third, asked whether he thinks importers would face reprisals if they didn't insist on Ross, says, "You said it. I didn't."

The Waterfront Commission of New York Harbor, a bi-state group formed in 1953 to combat crime and corruption, isn't so reticent. Ross charges "exorbitant rates" and its trucks aren't insulated to protect the fruit, says William P. Sirignano, the commission's executive director.

The commission is particularly interested in Ross' highest-paid employe, Pete DeFeo. Mr. Sirignano says the Federal Bureau of Investigation has described Mr. DeFeo as a member of the Mafia "family," or gang, of the late Vito Genovese, who directed Mafia activities in New York and New Jersey. The commission says Mr. DeFeo also is an associate of Gerardo Catena, overlord of organized crime in New Jersey.

Mr. DeFeo's brother-in-law, Frank Aquilino, founded Ross. Mr. Aquilino died in January 1969 and his widow and sons operate the company now. But the real power may lie with Mr. DeFeo, whose mug shot cropped up in a 1964 Senate committee report on racketeering.

Police records show Mr. DeFeo, 67, has had several encounters with the law, but no convictions. In 1947 he

was arrested on a homicide charge, but was found innocent. In 1965 he was arrested on a charge of disorderly
conduct, but was acquitted. In 1968 U.S. Attorney Robert Morgenthau obtained an indictment against Mr.
DeFeo and five others, charging they conspired to receive a kickback for arranging a $1.9 million loan from
a Teamsters Union pension fund to a New York builder.
The case hasn't yet come to trial.

The commission says it has stamped out much of
the gambling, loan-sharking and extortion that plagued
the waterfront before 1953. But now "criminals have
moved into fringe areas, including warehousing," says
Mr. Sirignano. He explains that he considers Ross a
warehouser, at least technically, because loaded Ross
trucks sometimes sit on the pier overnight before the
bananas are delivered.

He asserts that "it is obvious from the rapid and
tremendous growth" of Ross and a few other small
waterfront firms that these concerns "are part and par-
cel of the underworld's branching out into areas free
from any effective government control which would
protect the public interest."

Documents on file with the Interstate Commerce
Commission show that in 1968 Ross revenue was about
$429,000. That hardly qualifies the company as a busi-
ness giant. However, Ross earnings in 1968 totaled
about $89,000—a 21% profit margin that most blue-
chip companies might well envy.

Ross officials don't want to be interviewed. One in-
dicated over the phone that written questions would be
answered, so a list was promptly mailed. But no answers
were received.

Company headquarters at 219 Mulberry St., in a
drab working-class section on Manhattan's Lower East
Side, reinforces the impression that curious outsiders

aren't welcome. Black curtains cover the front windows of the office, which is in an old tenement.

The three big importers that unload at Port Newark and Pier 13 are Standard Fruit & Steamship Co., New Orleans; Pan American Fruit Co., New York; and West Indies Fruit Co., a subsidiary of Del Monte Corp., San Francisco. All speak highly of Ross.

One concern likes Ross because Ross trucks handle only bananas, "and not meat or fish or any obnoxious material to bananas, which could give bananas a bad odor," according to an official. This official says Ross never has attempted to coerce his firm into using Ross trucks.

"Years ago," an official at a second importer says, "we had a number of truckers doing our work. Some went out of business. Others didn't have decent equipment. Ross performs a good service."

The importers also argue that if competing truckers were allowed, costly tieups and traffic jams would result. However, United Fruit Co., Boston, the fourth major importer, allows competing truckers at its unloading operation, and observers say there are no traffic jams or long delays there. (United Fruit unloads at Weehawken, N.J. As a result of a Government antitrust suit, the company signed a consent decree in 1958 that, among other things, prohibited it from having an exclusive trucker like Ross.)

Some jobbers complain bitterly about Ross' hold on the two piers. "It costs me 22½ cents a box of bananas if Ross delivers," says one. "I could save 10 cents a box by sending my own truck down to the dock. But, no, I'm forced to use Ross."

Another jobber says he recently asked one of the three big importers why he couldn't use his own truck.

Recalls the jobber: "The importer said, 'This is the way it's got to be.' I say it smells."

One authoritative source maintains that the importers use only Ross because they "just don't want to take any chances." He explains: "They believe, rightly or wrongly, that Ross has connections. Nobody knows if Ross has connections with the Longshoremen's union, but I guess the importer feels that he shouldn't take a chance that his bananas will be mishandled on the pier."

A New York spokesman for the International Longshoreman's Association says he knows of no "dealings or connections" between the union and Ross.

But other jobbers say they like Ross, and insist they're saving money by using the company. Years ago, when a group of jobbers tried breaking Ross' grip by refusing to buy bananas at Port Newark, the effort collapsed when other jobbers continued buying there. One jobber argues that even though Ross trucks aren't insulated, bananas don't stay in the trucks long enough to be damaged by heat or cold.

Mr. Sirignano of the Waterfront Commission, however, cited Ross' "underworld connections" recently when he argued before a New Jersey legislative committee for passage of an anti-crime bill aimed at the New Jersey waterfront.

The bill passed. It requires licensing of warehouses and other pier facilities not now regulated by the Waterfront Commission. Under Mr. Sirignano's view that Ross is technically a warehouser, the trucking company, too, would have to get a license.

Denial of the license could hamper Ross operations. The commission says integrity and good character are among the yardsticks it uses to judge license applicants.

—STANLEY PENN

The Mob and a Drug Wholesaler

THE former vice president of a defunct drug wholesaler told a New York State inquiry into gangster operations in business of substantial clandestine payments of officials of a holding-company complex that controlled the drug concern for 21 months.

The executive, Benjamin Goldfinger, also told the New York State Investigation Commission that the holding company, identified as Twentieth Century Industries Inc. of Brooklyn, employed a former convict with links to the Mafia.

Twentieth Century Industries is a publicly held company. Its stock is traded over the counter.

Mr. Goldfinger said the drug wholesaler, Progressive Drug Inc. of the Bronx, N.Y., made the payments over a 21-month period while it was owned by a unit of Twentieth Century Industries. Twentieth Century Industries bought out the old-line drug wholesaler in January 1966 and sold it to a Canadian concern in October 1967. Progressive was put into bankruptcy proceedings a year after that.

The former official, who was granted immunity from prosecution to describe the payments in detail, said $18,925 was paid in 1966 to Martin Goldman, Twentieth Century Industries' vice president, and Larry Rosen, an employe of Mr. Hanger Inc., a Twentieth Century affiliate. The payment, he said, was made under the guise of travel and entertainment expenses for Henry Heinick and Lorence Press, principals of Pawnee Drug Inc., the Twentieth Century Industries unit that owned Progressive's stock.

Mr. Goldfinger said similar payments in 1967 totaled about $15,310.

Mr. Goldfinger said he kept a private record of each year's payments passed on to Messrs. Goldman and Rosen. Not until the end of the year, he said, were the payments listed under travel and entertainment.

He also told of $2,000 payments each made to Mr. Hanger's comptroller, Mr. Rosen and Samuel Goldman, president of Twentieth Century Industries and Martin Goldman's father.

Mr. Goldfinger said payments totalling $13,405 were made to Sal Metal Products Co. of Brooklyn, a Twentieth Century Industries subsidiary. And he said packages of unknown merchandise were sent for Mr. Press during 1966 and 1967 for which charges weren't made. Mr. Press later disputed the contention that charges hadn't been paid. He said some of the packages were sent to relatives and friends.

Mr. Goldfinger, who worked for Progressive for 40 years in moving up to vice president and comptroller, said the drug wholesaler had annual sales of about $10 million in 1967, while Twentieth Century Industries owned it. He said the company prior to Twentieth Century Industries' role didn't rely on outside financing to support its operations. After the holding company came in, however, outside financing charges grew to $7,000 or $8,000 a month, he stated.

He told the state inquiry that the company was a

losing operation before Twentieth Century Industries came in, chiefly because of product pilferage. After Twentieth Century became Progressive's owner, the pilferage stopped, but the company stayed in the red, he said.

Testimony by Mr. Goldfinger and other witnesses at the hearing also disclosed that Domenico "Nicky" Bando, described as an associate member of the Carlo Gambino Mafia family, was hired by Martin Goldman to guard Progressive Drug's warehouse. In addition to a weekly salary of about $150, according to the testimony, Bando was given $100 in cash each week "for good labor relations" which reportedly was "to be passed on downtown."

Bando pleaded guilty to charges in connection with the acid blinding of columnist Victor Riesel in 1956. He also served time in state and Federal prisons for selling narcotics.

According to Paul Kelly, assistant chief counsel for the state commission, putting Bando in charge of security at the warehouse, which contained narcotics, was like "putting the cat in the canary cage."

Bando, a short, slight, elderly man, invoked the Fifth Amendment 12 times in refusing to answer the commission's questions, including those about his alleged association with Progressive Drug.

Further testimony disclosed that Anniello "O'Neal" DellaCroce, described by law enforcement officials as a capo or acting boss, in the Carlo Gambino family due to Gambino's poor health, was employed at Royal Crown Bottling Co. of Newark, N.J., Inc., a Twentieth Century affiliate that formerly was a wholly owned subsidiary.

—BY A STAFF REPORTER

The Mob and Restaurants

TWO Brooklyn restaurant owners told the New York State Investigation Commission they signed labor contracts with a "paper" union whose only function seemed to be to collect dues.

One of the owners, identified only as Mr. C., said he didn't even inform his employes that he had signed a contract with the independent union, Local 26 of the Restaurant and Cafeteria Employes Union. He didn't want to burden them, he said. "They're good boys."

Mr. C., a slender frightened man who fidgeted with a rolled-up copy of Fortune magazine as he testified, said he started out 10 years ago paying $4 a month each for six employes, but the dues have since been raised to $5 a month. The number of employes assessed, he added, has always stayed at six, even though the restaurant has 15 to 20 workers. But, he declared, his employes never received union cards, union books or union benefits.

Two men identified as officials of the union also appeared at the hearing. One, Sam Browarnik, a beefy former convict who was identified as the union's secretary-treasurer, invoked the Fifth Amendment 40 times. John Amalfitano, another former convict who was identified as an organizer of the union, was allowed to leave without testifying because his attorney wasn't available.

Mr. C, in his testimony, said Amalfitano and another man visited the restaurant about 10 years ago to organize it. The second man handed him a calling card with the name "Gallo" written on it.

Later, one of the questions that Browarnik refused to answer was whether Joseph Gallo was an organizer of Local 26. Gallo, who currently is serving a seven to 14-year prison term for attempted extortion, has been identified as a well-known Brooklyn Mafia figure.

Mr. C said he asked who the Gallos were and was told that "their pedigree wasn't one of the highest." Under questioning, he said he was told "they are killers."

Asked if there were any changes in the restaurant's treatment of its employes since the union contract was signed, Mr. C replied: "None whatsoever. We just keep giving our employes what they deserve for what they produce, and they seem very happy."

Mr. C said the restaurant signed up with the union because "it was the American way of doing things," and admitted the initial contract was signed without the knowledge of the restaurant's employes.

The other Brooklyn restaurant owner, Mr. B, who also requested anonymity, told how Amalfitano organized his employes. After he refused to sign up, his restaurant was picketed for two or three months by strangers, he said. After he got a court injunction to stop the picketing, Mr. B testified, all the restaurant's windows were broken.

Mr. B says he usually has seven to nine employes, though employment can run as high as 15 or 16 on holidays. However, he added, he pays union dues of $5 each for eight employes regardless of the number actually employed.

Asked about benefits derived from signing up with

the union, Mr. B said he got "peace" and "the respect of the union," in that other unions recognize that he has a union shop.

Paul Bellantuono, a cook at a Brooklyn restaurant, told the commission that three or four years ago he was told by his boss that he belonged to a union. But, he added, "I don't remember the number of the union or the name." He said he never received a card, attended a meeting, received notification of a meeting or paid dues. Mr. Bellantuono did identify an application for membership to Local 26 made out in his writing. The application wasn't signed.

Two waiters, former members of Local 26, said union dues were deducted from their pay. However, they added, they didn't receive any benefits from union membership because they weren't sick.

—BY A STAFF REPORTER

The Mob and a Night Club

BENJAMIN Maksik still boasts that the Town & Country Club in Brooklyn that he built from a hot-dog stand "was the largest nightclub in the world," with an entertainment roster that read like a who's who of show business.

The club, which opened its doors in 1955, closed in 1968 from lack of business.

Mr. Maksik told the New York Investigation Commission about the period leading up to the time in 1957 when "it came to me like a dream one night that there was an attempt being made to take over my place."

Two weeks later, after the notorious meeting of Mafia chieftains at Apalachin, N.Y., Mr. Maksik understood. "I realized that 80% of the people I was doing business with were connected with (Apalachin)," he said.

Mr. Maksik testified that through a man called Joseph Gulmi, also known as Joe Miller, he engaged a labor relations firm, SGS Associates. The firm's initials stood for Saltzstein, Gambino and Schiller, Mr. Maksik said, and Carlo Gambino, who has been identified as heading a Brooklyn Mafia family, was one of the consultants.

While Mr. Maksik admitted that his labor troubles didn't improve with the hiring of SGS, he kept them on the payroll until mid-1958 and paid them $12,500.

Mr. Gulmi, whom the state commission has unsuccessfully attempted to subpoena, continued at the club as SGS's "eyes and ears," Mr. Maksik said.

Next, he testified, Mr. Gulmi suggested that Town & Country switch meat suppliers. He suggested Emcee Meat Co., a Brooklyn supplier. While the first shipment from Emcee was short-weighted, Mr. Maksik said, the prices "were significantly better" and he kept them.

Emcee Meat, Mr. Maksik said, was headed by Paul Castellano, identified by law enforcement authorities as a member of Carlo Gambino's Brooklyn family. Though the meat was "a little inferior," Mr. Maksik said, "I thought I could get by."

Meanwhile, Mr. Gulmi, whom the commission's assistant counsel, Peter R. O'Connell, called a "ubiquitous operator," put Town & Country in touch with Mafia-controlled shortening, fuel, laundry supply and liquor firms, Mr. Maksik testified.

One day, when his financial woes were worse than usual, Mr. Maksik said, Mr. Gulmi, who the commission says has two bookmaking convictions, again approached him.

"One day Joe came over and said, 'I know you need money. You're a nice guy. We love you. How much do you want?" Mr. Maksik recalled.

Mr. Maksik said that, under Mr. Gulmi's pressuring, he replied facetiously, "As much as you can give me."

The next day, Mr. Maksik said, Mr. Gulmi deposited a paper grocery bag containing $70,000 in cash on his desk. Mr. Gulmi, he said, wouldn't take a note for the money, nor would he take it back. "He said it was legitimate money," Mr. Maksik said.

In 1958, Mr. Maksik said, Town & Country filed for court protection under Chapter 11 of the Federal Bankruptcy law. The day the proceedings were published, Mr. Maksik testified, Mr. Gulmi demanded the $70,000.

Mr. Maksik said he made a deal with Mr. Gulmi stipulating that it would be paid back in $10,000 instalments. The cash, he testified, was delivered to Mr. Gulmi by his wife's uncle, who took a bag containing $10,000 to Mr. Gulmi every Sunday at the corner of Flatbush Avenue and Avenue U in Brooklyn.

Mr. Gulmi also offered to "fix" Mr. Maksik's problems with the Internal Revenue Service, the former nightclub owner testified. The cost would be "$40,000, $50,000 or $60,000," he said.

Mr. Maksik said that about three to four months before it happened, Mr. Gulmi said a certain IRS agent would look over the club's books and assess him for $300,000 in excise taxes.

"Every word he said came true," Mr. Maksik said. "I was in a state of shock thereafter."

Mr. Maksik said that he eventually was assessed for about $800,000 in excise taxes by the IRS. He added that he currently owes $230,000 to $250,000 and that he's making monthly payments.

In the beginning, Mr. Maksik told the commission, he thought Mr. Gulmi was a bookmaker. In 1955, after the club opened, he noticed him in the club every day making a number of telephone calls. Eventually, Mr. Gulmi identified himself as a representative of the bakers' union, Mr. Maksik said.

Mr. O'Connell called Mr. Gulmi "a mysterious racket figure" who, "by using a variety of methods and techniques, gained influence and, in some instances, a measure of control in a number of businesses in the metropolitan area."

—BY A STAFF REPORTER

The Mob and a Plastics Company

THE chief executive of a publicly held Long Island concern paid out $458,000 and 65,000 shares of company stock for protection "to keep the hoodlums of Long Island off my back," according to testimony given the New York State Investigation Commission.

A substantial part of the funds paid by Maurice Minuto, chairman and president of Nylo-Thane Plastics Corp., Farmingdale, N.Y., were lent him by Royal National Bank, New York.

According to testimony and commission evidence, $292,000 and 25,000 Nylo-Thane shares went to John Masiello who directed Mr. Minuto to the bank for a loan after $25,000 had been extorted from the executive at gunpoint.

Masiello was identified by Paul D. Kelly, the commission's assistant chief counsel, as a prominent loan shark in the New York area who previously had "milked" J. S. Wald & Co., a trucker.

"The loans were no more than a subterfuge to get money from the bank for Mr. John Masiello," Mr. Kelly charged.

William Goldfine, chairman and president of Royal National, told the commission that he didn't know Masiello was a racketeer. He added that Masiello, who owns Setmar Holding Corp., New York, has been a depositor for many years. Mr. Goldfine also said that he had "no idea" that Masiello was benefiting from Royal National's loans to Mr. Minuto, his company or companies owned by Mr. Minuto.

During his testimony, Mr. Goldfine disclosed that the Small Business Administration has loaned Masiello $466,000 for his companies.

Later, Masiello invoked the Fifth Amendment when Mr. Kelly asked him whether he had used any of the SBA funds for loansharking.

Nylo-Thane makes a chemical additive designed to accelerate the curing of rubber. In December 1967, after its stock had risen to a high of $85 bid, the company admitted that it had never made a cent.

Earlier in 1967, a Federal court enjoined the company, its previous president, Mr. Minuto and his wife, and a financial consultant from further violations of antifraud provisions of the securities laws in Nylo-Thane stock or other issues.

The SEC's complaint alleged that the defendants committed violations in connection with the sale of common stock of Nylo-Thane by offering circulars, containing misleading statements about the company's product.

According to Mr. Minuto's testimony, his troubles began on Aug. 16, 1967, when a man identified as Allan Morrell telephoned the executive to inform him that he knew someone who was interested in purchasing some unregistered Nylo-Thane stock as an investment.

At 7:30 that night, Mr. Minuto testified, Mr. Morrell, a hoodlum identified as Julius Klein and five or six other men showed up at his office. Two of the men carried knives and one had a revolver with a silencer, Mr.

Minuto testified. Klein currently is serving a five-to-six year sentence for grand larceny.

According to Mr. Minuto, Klein demanded a $25,-000 corporate check, and threatened that Mr. Minuto's wife and children would be killed if he went to the police. Mr. Minuto signed a check, he testified, and one of the men with Klein forged the cosignature of Louis R. Braunston, the company's former president. Mr. Morrell stood by and did nothing, he said. After being held captive all night at a motel, Mr. Minuto cashed the check the next morning and turned over the $25,000 in cash to Klein's men.

Later that day, Mr. Minuto tried to borrow $25,000 to cover the loss from Masiello, the executive testified. Previously, he said, he had borrowed $4,000 to $5,000 from Masiello's Setmar Holding through Thomas McKeever, an ex-convict who manages the holding company's ANR Leasing Corp., a car and truck leasing concern.

Masiello told Mr. Minuto he didn't have $25,000 and sent him to Royal National for a loan, the executive testified. According to commission records, the bank loaned $50,000 to Nylo-Thane on Aug. 28, 1967. Commission records also show that Nylo-Thane wrote two checks to Setmar totaling $49,000 shortly thereafter. In addition, on Aug. 24, 1967, 25,000 shares of Nylo-Thane stock, then valued at $500,000, were transferred from Mr. Minuto's wife, Olanda, to Setmar, the commission's evidence showed.

According to his testimony, Mr. Minuto turned over the $49,000 and 25,000 shares to Masiello for protection from Long Island's hoodlums. He said he never saw Klein again.

According to commission records, Masiello and his son, John Jr., received another $38,000 from Mr. Minuto between November 1967 and May 1968. The only repayment from Masiello, $13,500, was made in late 1967.

In August 1968, Mr. Minuto borrowed $350,000 from Royal National as loans to Carlon Construction Inc. and Dorian Cosmetic Corp., two "shell" companies he owns, and as a personal loan to himself. These loans, according to commission records and subsequent testimony, were secured with fidelity bonds issued by State Fire & Casualty Corp., Miami, which was ordered by Florida authorities to stop doing business in December 1968.

In November 1968, Royal National loaned Mr. Minuto $100,000 on a paid-up $100,000 life insurance policy that he obtained from Community Life Insurance Co. of Oklahoma, the commission said. Royal National also loaned Mr. Minuto $15,000 the month before, according to the commission.

The cost of the fidelity bonds, the life insurance and collateral to obtain the loans totaled $35,000 and 35,000 Nylo-Thane shares, the commission said. The stock then was valued at about $700,000.

The fidelity bonds and insurance policy were obtained for Mr. Minuto by Emil "Tommy" Tucker, owner of the now defunct Lime Investment Corp. Tucker, under questioning, admitted he has been convicted for forgery and grand larceny, among other things.

Subsequently, according to commission evidence, Mr. Minuto, Carlon Construction and Dorian Cosmetics paid ANR a total of $181,000 in related transactions. There also were payments of $9,000 to Mrs. Elizabeth Masiello and $15,000 to John Masiello Jr.

Mr. Minuto also sent a total of $45,000 to the Flamingo and Circus casinos in Las Vegas before a trip there in late November which, according to the commission, was used to pay off the pre-existing debt of a known gambler.

During the trip, which he took with John Masiello Jr., Mr. Minuto lost another $30,000 gambling, the commission said. Mr. Minuto's $35,000 personal certificate of deposit at Royal National also served as collateral for an ANR obligation, the commission said. Finally, according to the commission, interest and discounts on the loans Mr. Minuto received in order to pay off Masiello and others cost him $9,000.

Mr. Minuto and Royal National's Mr. Goldfine also testified to Mr. Minuto's donation of 5,000 Nylo-Thane shares at a testimonial dinner for Mr. Goldfine. The shares subsequently were turned over to Mr. Goldfine's favorite charity, the Hebrew Home for the Aged, Riverdale, N.Y. Masiello, Mr. Goldfine said, was at the dinner because, "He's always been interested in the home."

—BY A STAFF REPORTER

The Mob and Small Business

TESTIMONY at a House committee hearing disclosed still another possible conduit through which Federal aid to small business may have flowed into a Mafia-linked trucking company.

The chairman of the alleged conduit, New York-based Kenrich Corp., denied that Federal money was used in the transaction at issue, however.

Kenrich has received $700,000 in financing from Royal Business Funds Corp., a Federally licensed and funded small business investment company. Through a loan company in the complex of concerns that it controls, Kenrich had provided $450,000 in loans to ANR Leasing Corp., a Bronx, N.Y., trucking concern that at the time was controlled by John A. Masiello Sr.

Masiello, who has been identified by law enforcement agencies as a Mafia member, his son, John Jr., and ANR are among defendants recently indicted on charges of bribery and conspiring to defraud the Post Office Department in connection with a truck-leasing plan.

The Masiellos and their companies also have been identified as receiving cash and stock payments from a Long Island executive anxious to be free of extortion demands from hoodlums. The New York State investigation commission more than once has identified the elder Masiello as a leading New York area loan shark.

ANR previously was shown to have benefited from $560,000 in direct Small Business Administration loans and from two SBICs—one of them Royal Business Funds. The hearing, before the House Banking Committee, was the first of several Congressional inquiries expected in the ANR case.

Rep. Reuss (D., Wis.) introduced the name of Kenrich, noting that Delaware Valley Financial Corp., a company Kenrich controls, loaned money to ANR in 1967, after Kenrich received its financing from Royal Business Funds.

Mr. Reuss charged that these transactions involved relending of SBIC funds, an action prohibited by SBA regulations. Asked by Mr. Reuss if he agreed with this analysis, Arthur Singer, SBA associate administrator in charge of the investment company program, replied: "It appears that is correct." Following the hearing, Mr. Singer said the agency is looking closely at the Royal Business Funds-Kenrich-ANR relationship, but is still tracing the route followed by the SBIC funds in this instance.

Prior to the hearing, Martin Wright, Kenrich chairman, said the Royal Business Funds financing was completely absorbed by the cash needs of Laribee Wire Inc., a wire and plastics manufacturer then 60% owned by Kenrich. None of the SBIC money ever flowed to Delaware Valley, then a wholly owned subsidiary of Laribee, he said.

As Mr. Wright described it, commercial loans to ANR were arranged by Norman J. Wiener, a commercial lending specialist with finance company operations of his own. Mr. Wiener was brought in to head Delaware Valley in 1964. Prior to that Delaware Valley had been a consumer loan firm. However, Mr. Wiener said in a separate interview that through his Worth Financial Corp., which became a Delaware Valley subsidiary, he had enjoyed a "very profitable" business financing Masiello trucking companies since 1962. Mr. Wiener said that until early in 1969 he was totally unaware of Masiello's underworld connections.

In a complicated series of stock and cash exchanges, Kenrich bought out Mr. Wiener's interest in the consumer operations, leaving him with control of the commercial loans, Mr. Wright says. These include the ANR debt, which now totals about $350,000 in principal and accrued interest, according to Mr. Wiener. At the same time, though, Mr. Wiener continues as senior vice president of a new company, Laribee Credit Corp., a subsidiary of Laribee Wire Inc. Laribee Credit, according to a March proxy statement issued by Laribee Wire, will take over the operations of Delaware Valley, though curtailing the commercial lending activities.

It previously had been disclosed that Greater New York Capital Corp., an SBIC owned by Mr. Wiener and his father, independently loaned ANR $50,000 in 1966 —a debt on which payments have been in arrears since 1967. Greater New York Capital currently is paying off, at the SBA's request, $300,000 it borrowed from Uncle Sam.

Although it didn't come up at the hearing, still another thread in the ANR matter is a currently inactive company, Bermer Leasing Corp., New York. Bermer was formed by an associate of Mr. Wiener to take over the ANR Post Office truck leases that are involved in the fraud charges. Bert Brodsky, the owner of Bermer said he proposed to postal authorities to use the ANR trucks to carry on the Government contract after Masiello's arrangement fell through.

Bermer never succeeded in its objective, but it continues to carry a $420,000 debt to Royal National Bank that ANR owned originally but transferred to Bermer, Mr. Brodsky says. These transactions, it's understood, also are receiving Federal scrutiny.

Royal National Bank is affiliated through stock interest and common directorships with Royal Business Funds. It also participated with the SBA in direct loans to ANR.

The committee hearing, under Chairman Patman (D., Texas), also brought to light some of the oversights within the SBA that allowed the Masiello firm to obtain its initial Federal assistance in the form of a $350,000 direct loan in 1965.

For reasons still unclear, Royal National Bank's application for the second loan of Federal funds for ANR, totaling $300,000, listed Mrs. Elizabeth Masiello, wife of John Sr., as a 70% owner. However, on the next line of the application, where those holding 20% or more of the voting stock are supposed to be listed, Mrs. Masiello's name didn't appear. The three names that were listed included her son and an ex-convict, Thomas McKeever, shown as vice president and general manager.

In line with regular SBA practices, the agency's New York office only passed the three names from this line along to Washington for security clearance. SBA officials testified that the names in turn were sent to the Federal Bureau of Investigation, which failed to detect McKeever's jail record. (John Masiello Jr. subsequently was charged with manslaughter and maiming in connection with a Yonkers, N.Y., tavern fight in which one elderly businessman died and another lost an eye, but is still awaiting trial on the charges, Chairman Patman said in his remarks.)

In late 1966 a New York bank employe—who got

his information from back copies of the New York Times—tipped the SBA to the fact that it had made a loan to a Mafia-connected firm. The following January, though, on intra-agency memorandum to then-SBA Administrator Bernard L. Boutin recommended against seeking recovery of the loan because of dubious legal grounds.

The memo commented, "It appears that the FBI missed the boat on name check." But, it added, "bringing the matter into court could prove embarrassing to the Department of Justice and SBA."

The memo stated that the FBI wanted the SBA to continue efforts to obtain detailed financial statements from the Masiellos "and thereby possibly obtain useful information for the Justice Department." The SBA witnesses at the hearing conceded that they never followed through with the needed information. Nor did they discover that ANR had become delinquent on its loan payments almost immediately—information that would have provided a legal basis for seeking recovery.

Arthur D. Horner, director of the SBA's Office of Audits and Investigations, sought to soften the impact of the memo by saying the agency failed to provide the FBI with adequate information to identify McKeever.

—BY A STAFF REPORTER

Who's to Blame?

ON a recent television show, Jimmy Breslin, author-humorist, was poking fun at Newark's crime scandals, saying, "Newark is so bad it's giving the Mafia there a bad name." Listening but not finding it funny was Milford Vieser, a business leader in Newark and a top official of Mutual Benefit Life Insurance, who recalls with annoyance, "All those viewers were watching and thinking Newark is just a joke."

If Newark is a joke, the business community is partly to blame.

Crime investigators maintain that some Newark business executives aid in the spread of organized crime by closing their eyes to Mafia-run, illegal gambling rackets operating in plants and offices. Some businessmen, it's contended, give respectability to the mobsters by consorting and having business dealings with them. Concerning widespread charges of graft in Newark's city administration, a former Federal investigator in the Garden State reminds, "It takes two to make a bribe, the city official who accepts it, and the businessman who gives it."

The businessman, of course, isn't the chief culprit. Often he is an unwilling victim. The main villains in the Newark drama appear to be some public officials, who have been charged with taking graft to augment their incomes, and Mafia racketeers, who, to protect their illegal rackets, make payoffs to public officials. Federal grand juries in Newark have brought indictments against 15, including Mayor Hugh J. Addonizio, on charges of accepting kickbacks, and against 55, including Mafia chieftain Simone (Sam the Plumber) DeCavalcante, on charges of illegal gambling activities.

Yet the businessman shows indifference when he has a chance to combat the rackets. Brendan Byrne, a former Newark prosecutor, conducted investigations against illegal gambling. He says he was once reprimanded by a highly-respected businessman for his efforts. against the mob. "He cautioned me that Newark has to put its best foot forward, and if I make these disclosures it'll give the city a black eye."

Mr. Byrne says $50 million yearly is the take from numbers and bookmaking in Newark. The profits from the operations are funneled by mobsters into loansharking and other rackets as well as into legitimate businesses.

Gambling is popular in the plants. Some business executives worry that attempts to curtail the betting might provoke slowdowns or strikes. John Stamler, assistant prosecutor in Elizabeth, N.J., says the head of a small concern near Newark was greatly annoyed at the police for arresting his foreman for bookmaking activities in the plant. "The president of the firm had known for years the foreman had been taking book, but his only concern was when the foreman would be out on bail so he could be back on the job," Mr. Stamler says.

Says Frederick W. Lacey, new U.S. Attorney in New Jersey, "The plant manager is all too often discouraged by his superiors about stopping shop stewards from openly and brazenly taking bets or accepting numbers. I'd take much comfort from action by businessmen designed to shut down all gambling in their plants and buildings."

Mr. Lacey, who charged in a speech that "organized crime is taking us over," hits out at businessmen for dealing with underworld figures. He cites the recent action of a grand jury in nearby Union County in condemning builders of an apartment complex in Parsippany, N.J., for using services of Mafia bosses to assure labor peace during construction.

According to the grand jury, the builders agreed to pay $70,000 to the late Nick Delmore, a Mafioso who died in 1964, and continued payments to Delmore's successor, Sam DeCavalcante. In return, the builders, by using largely non-union labor, saved $2,000 per apartment unit—an overall savings of $1.3 million in construction costs, the grand jury said. It found disturbing, the grand jury added, the "cooperation of businessmen in paying tribute to reputed criminals."

The business-social ties that some executives maintain with mobsters disturb Federal officials. Philip Dameo, president and chief stockholder of Peoples Express Co., a local trucking firm, is said by a business acquaintance of his to be well liked and to have a good reputation. Active in civic affairs, Mr. Dameo is a founder and vice president of the 200 Club, a Newark group that raises money for wives of policemen and firemen killed in the line of duty.

Even so, Mr. Dameo has said he was associated with Gerardo (Jerry) Catena when Mr. Dameo bought into Peoples Express in 1946. He told a hearing of the Interstate Commerce Commission in 1967 that Catena sold out his interest in 1952, but that he still sees him socially. Catena is described by law enforcement officials as New Jersey's top Mafia chieftain, successor to the late Vito Genovese gang.

Consider Valentine Electric Co., a contracting firm that does construction work in Newark. Government officials have said a principal figure in Valentine is Anthony (Tony Boy) Boiardo, a Mafioso, and son of aging racketeer Ruggiero (Richie the Boot) Boiardo. Tony Boy is a defendant with Mayor Addonizio on the extortion charge indictment.

Despite Boiardo's alleged influence in Valentine, developers blithely use the firm for electrical wiring in construction work. One businessman, who is employing Valentine's services now, argues why shouldn't he use the firm inasmuch as Valentine hasn't been charged with any wrongdoing. Besides, the businessman adds, Valentine was low bidder for this particular job. "Valentine is the best subcontractor of that type in northern New Jersey," this businessman maintains.

The Greater Newark Chamber of Commerce, which lists Valentine and Peoples Express as members, recently launched an investigation to determine if either concern is controlled by organized crime. Charles J. Hall, president of the Chamber of Commerce, warns his group will take certain unspecified action if it is found to the chamber's satisfaction that criminal elements control either company and refuse to sell out. Efforts to reach Valentine and Peoples Express about this matter were unsuccessful.

It takes courage for a businessman to publicly expose what is going on. Many don't want to stick their necks out. Also, refusal to yield to the demands of the underworld may lead to financial ruin. A law enforcement investigator tells about the head of a trucking firm based near Newark who wouldn't make payoffs demanded by a corrupt Teamster chief.

"This businessman was subjected to organized harassment," the investigator reports. "His drivers (members of a local union controlled by the Teamster chief) began encountering all sorts of "delays"—6 to 8 hours for deliveries instead of 3. Trucks failing to make pickups at the dock. Drivers refusing to work overtime. This man had a fleet of 47 trucks. Because of all the harassment, he was taking home less than $10,000 a year."

The businessman who must pay graft in order to obtain contracts from the city administration sees himself as a victim of circumstances. Says a former Justice Department sleuth: "The businessman thinks that graft is the American way of life. Also, he is in a competitive situation, and he's isolated. He doesn't know what his competitor will do. If the city official says the contract is going to cost X amount of dollars, he figures his competitor would be willing to go along, so he'd better pay it."

Some of Newark's business leaders say they are hopeful the current investigations that U.S. Attorney Lacey is spearheading will clear the air. "Maybe this will be the trigger that will set off a movement for better government," says Donald MacNaughton, president of Prudential Insurance Co., headquartered in Newark. "Maybe more of the citizens will get involved."

Mr. Lacey says business leaders must overcome their apathy. "Where there is a substantial sentiment that the government of a city isn't performing honestly, the business community should look for candidates that are clean, decent and incorruptible," he says. "They should support such candidates not only financially, but with the manpower needed to run for office, even at the risk of retribution from political forces."

The business community in Newark hasn't pushed hard in the past for clean city government. Take Mayor Addonizio as an example. Though Newark's Chamber of Commerce recently declared its "shock" at the mayor's indictment, and demanded that Mr. Addonizio be removed from office, the charges against the mayor came as no real shock to many of the executives whose firms are members of the chamber.

Many of these executives had backed Mr. Addonizio in his successful 1966 campaign for a second term despite widespread suspicion then of corruption at City Hall and despite a Newark grand jury's public condemnation of the police force in 1965 for its alleged failure to crack down against illegal gambling.

In defense, a Newark businessman says, "Addonizio was always responsive to any legitimate request that business made." Another businessman maintains that even if the suspicion of corruption existed, "there's a grand jury for that sort of thing." This businessman adds: "If I were mayor I'd know a thousand ways of giving trouble to somebody who gave me a screwing by not backing me for reelection. Why should we be heroes?"

Most of the city's business leaders live in the surrounding suburbs and therefore don't have the incentive to push actively for a clean government in Newark. One who performed an active role was Robert Lilley, president until recently of Newark-based New Jersey Telephone Co. Mr. Lilley headed the commission created by then Gov. Hughes to handle the delicate task of investigating the causes of Newark's 1967 race riot. That commission showed courage when it charged that a factor leading to the bitterness in the Negro wards was a belief that the city administration was corrupt. Newark recently lost Mr. Lilley when the parent company, American Telephone & Telegraph Co., promoted him to executive vice president and transferred him to its New York headquarters.

It's not just the business leaders who have fled to the suburbs. "The white middle-class in Newark is almost nonexistent," says a liberal Catholic lawyer who lives and works in the city and is active in local politics. "It's not like New York with its substantial Jewish middle and upper middle-class interested in decent government."

"The only middle-class in Newark to speak of is Italian. Unfortunately, there's a tremendous amount of bitterness between the blacks and Italians. If a moderate, intelligent Italian from the middle-class came forward, it would be to the city's benefit. So far there's nobody except Imperiale." The reference is to Councilman Anthony Imperiale, a white militant heartily disliked by Newark's Negroes.

It remains to be seen if coming elections will lead to a better city government. But regardless of their outcome, it already seems clear that when the Mafia makes inroads, the business community is likely to bear some of the blame.

—STANLEY PENN

OTHER TITLES FROM DOW JONES BOOKS

TED WILLIAMS,
SAM THE GENIUS
and Other Sports Stories
from The Wall Street Journal
192 pages
Soft cover, $1.95
There's a rumor among sports fans that the best sports writing in America can be found on the front page of The Wall Street Journal. That would be the last place a lot of sports fans would think to look, but to the Journal's three million readers, the talk isn't surprising. Some 30 of these stories, probing the business and human sides and the serious and funny moments in sports, are compiled here. 1970.

THE JILTED AARDVARK
and Other Improbable Tales
from The Wall Street Journal
110 pages
Soft cover, $1.95
Meant mainly to entertain, these 32 stories from the front page of The Journal include tales about the monkey that escaped in the airport; the poodle that didn't like his luxury doghouse; the stunt cyclist who can count to 20 before the anesthesia takes hold; Charles Atlas, who did have sand kicked in his face; and many more. 1970.

BUSINESS AND BLACKS
by the editors of The Wall Street Journal
150 pages
Soft cover, $1.95
This collection of articles from The Wall Street Journal relates the accomplishments and the disappointments in the attempts of the most important institutions in the country to "blend the racial minorities into the melting pot." What has been attempted, and how well? How have the minorities reacted? In short, how are things going? 1970.

OUR MISTREATED WORLD
by the editors of The Wall Street Journal
207 pages
Soft cover, $1.95
This is not a cheerful book. It is a collection of articles about how we have mistreated our physical world— how we have polluted its air and its rivers, littered its landscapes with junked cars and coal-mine waste heaps, slaughtered its wild creatures and threatened to destroy even ourselves with poisons of our own making. 1970.

CHARLES H. DOW: ECONOMIST
edited by George W. Bishop, Jr.
307 pages
Hard cover, $9.50
A selection of his writings on business cycles. His editorials represent one of the earliest efforts to analyze the periodic ups and downs of the economy. The editorials collected, written around the turn of the century, illustrate the depth and calibre of Dow's work on business.

THE DOW JONES
INVESTOR'S HANDBOOK
edited by Maurice L. Farrell
120-140 pages, Soft cover
Convenient reference to stock and bond market indicators. Complete Dow Jones Averages through the end of the year prior to publication; individual records of common and preferred stocks listed on the New York and American Stock Exchanges (1969 edition on includes National Stock Exchange), showing the year's range of prices, net change, volume, and dividend, plus the year's most active issues; more than 2000 over-the-counter quotations (beginning in the 1970 edition); and articles of interest to the investor by the editors of The Wall Street Journal and Barron's
1966 edition, $1.85 + 15 cents postage
1968 edition, $1.85 + 15 cents postage
1969 edition, $2.45 + 15 cents postage
1970 edition, $2.60
1971 edition, $2.60

DOW JONES BOOKS, P.O. BOX 300, PRINCETON, NEW JERSEY 08540